Lunch Bags!

25 HANDMADE SACKS & WRAPS TO SEW TODAY

stashBOOKS

an imprint of C&T Publishing

Text and artwork copyright © 2010 by by C&T Publishing, Inc.

Publisher: Amy Marson

Creative Director: Gailen Runge

Acquisitions Editor: Susanne Woods

Editors: Ann Haley and Cynthia Bix

Technical Editor: Ann Haley

Copyeditor/Proofreader: Wordfirm Inc.

Cover/Book Designer: Kristen Yenche

Design Director: Kristy Zacharias

Production Coordinator: Zinnia Heinzmann

Production Editor: Julia Cianci

Illustrator: Mary Flynn

Photography by Christina Carty-Francis and Diane Pedersen of C&T Publishing, Inc., unless otherwise noted

Published by Stash Books an imprint of C&T Publishing, Inc., P.O. Box 1456, Lafayette, CA 94549

Library of Congress Cataloging-in-Publication Data

Lunch bags! : 25 handmade sacks & wraps to sew today / by C&T Publishing.

    p. cm.

ISBN 978-1-60705-004-9 (soft cover)

1. Tote bags. 2. Bags. 3. Sewing. 4. C&T Publishing. I. Title.

TT667.L96 2010

646.4'8--dc22

                              2009051364

Printed in China

10 9 8 7 6 5 4 3 2 1

Contents

Introduction

In my quest to be an environmentally friendly, nonbranded mom who prides herself on creating more unique versions of store-bought items for herself and her family, I decided to make my preschooler a lunch bag. While I searched all the usual places, I struggled to find any inspiring patterns, but I did find a wonderful selection on etsy.com available for purchase. As the acquisitions editor for Stash Books and C&T Publishing, I feel sure that many people share the same values regarding reducing and reusing, and I have confidence that some simple sewing skills can provide the solution to bypassing the ordinary store-bought selection of lunch bags and choosing to create unique and personal projects.

This book represents the work of some of the most talented designers working with fabrics and includes detailed patterns for the lunch bags they have created. Within these pages you will find simple bags suitable for adding personalization and embellishments, sophisticated bags to take to the office, children's bags for school or picnics, and even a bit of crochet! This is the second book in a series of titles called The Design Collective. I have invited this clever group of artists who have taken the possibilities of the humble piece of cloth (whether it be laminated cotton, washable nylon, or canvas) to amazing levels to share one of her fabulous designs in our book. Each of the contributors provides detailed instructions for her individual techniques. Some of the projects are simple and can be customized based on fabric choices alone, and some are a bit more of a challenge, but all are enjoyable, environmentally friendly, practical creations. I hope you enjoy making and gifting these bags for yourself, friends, and family.

Susanne Woods

I have always had a love for crafts, thanks to my grandmother, who taught me to be creative as a child. My main passion is sewing. There is just something amazing about cutting up fabric, sewing it together, and watching as it takes shape into something you have created. Most of what I make is inspired by my daughter, such as this lunch bag. I had been looking for an alternative to store-bought lunch pails and needed something to keep her food cold and that could be easily cleaned, all while still looking trendy.

www.ziggystitch.etsy.com

MADE BY
Chrystalleena Beauchamp

Keep Your Lunch Cool Bag

Finished size: 8″ × 8″ × 7″

Keeping it cool is what this bag is all about—insulated and lined with wipe-clean nylon for taking care of spills. The bag is thoughtfully designed with a long shoulder strap and an elasticized bottle holder to keep everything in its place.

MATERIALS AND CUTTING INSTRUCTIONS

See illustrations on page 8 for patterns A and C. Pattern B can be found on page 122.

⅝ yard home decor fabric for outer shell:

- Cut 1 of pattern A for bag shell; note hook-and-loop tape placement and dots for alignment.
- Cut 2 of pattern B for bag sides; transfer dots for alignment and strap placement.
- Cut 1 of pattern C for flap.
- Cut 1 strip 2″ × 32″ for strap.

½ yard fabric for inside flap and straps:

- Cut 1 of pattern C for flap facing.
- Cut 1 strip 2″ × 32″ for strap.
- Cut 3 strips 2″ × 7″ for drink holder straps.

⅝ yard lining or nylon fabric for lining:

- Cut 1 of pattern A for shell lining. Alignment dots should be marked ¼″ from edge where shown in illustration below.
- Cut 2 of pattern B for lining sides; transfer dots for alignment.
- Cut 1 square 8″ × 8″ for ice pocket.

⅝ yard Insul~Brite insulation

⅝ yard cotton batting:

- Cut 1 each of batting and Insul~Brite pattern A for bag.
- Cut 2 each of batting and Insul~Brite pattern B for sides.
- Cut 1 each of batting and Insul~Brite pattern C for flap.

15″ (¼″ wide) braided elastic:

- Cut into 3 pieces 5″ each for drink holder straps.

5″ (¾″ wide) sew-on hook-and-loop tape:

- Cut 1 piece hook-and-loop tape 2″ in length for ice pocket.
- Cut 1 piece hook-and-loop tape 3″ in length for outer flap.

Quilting basting spray

Fabric pencil or other fabric-safe marking device

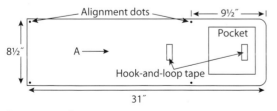

Patterns A and C

CONSTRUCTION

Note: *All seam allowances are ¼″.*

Assembling the Lining

Ice Pocket

1. Fold over one side of the 8″ × 8″ lining square by ½″ and press. Fold over another ½″, press again, and then stitch ¼″ from the folded edge. Repeat for the other 3 sides.

2. Center a 2″ piece of hook-and-loop tape on the wrong side of the pocket 1¼″ from the top edge. Sew all 4 edges of one side of the hook-and-loop tape.

3. Place the pocket on the lining A near the curved end. Position the other side of the hook-and-loop tape to the right side of lining A, so it lines up with the piece on the pocket, and stitch all 4 edges of the hook-and-loop tape.

4. Pin the pocket to the lining, with the wrong side of the pocket facing the right side of the lining.

5. Start sewing at the pocket's opening along the hem lines on the pocket front. Sew 3 sides, leaving the top (near the hook-and-loop tape) open to form the pocket.

Drink Straps

1. Fold a 2″ × 7″ drink strap in half lengthwise, right sides together.

2. Sew the long raw edges of the drink strap together. Trim the seam allowance.

3. Turn the fabric right side out. Use a safety pin as needed to help turn the fabric.

4. Insert the elastic through the hole. You will need to stretch the elastic so that you can pull it through the other end of the fabric.

5. Sew a strap to the front lining of side B, as indicated on the pattern. Make sure the strap seam is facing the lining. (**Note**: *The easiest way to do this is with 2 safety pins. Safety pin one side of the elastic—that has been pulled through fabric—and line it up with the first dot. Pin the other end of the elastic in place using the second safety pin; then sew, leaving both pins in place. Remove safety pins. The further you pull the elastic, the tighter the finished strap will be.*)

6. Repeat Steps 1–5 for the remaining 2 straps, using the pattern dots for placement.

Lining

1. Pin lining A and one lining B piece together, lining up the dots with right sides together, and sew.

2. Pin lining A and the remaining lining B side piece together, lining up the dots with right sides together. Sew. (**Note**: *When attaching the second lining B side, do not sew between the lines. This opening will be used to turn the bag later.*)

Assembling the Outer Shell

Outer Shell

1. Pin one side of the 3″ piece of hook-and-loop tape to fabric front A, as indicated on the illustration (page 8). Sew in place.

2. Using quilting basting spray, spray the wrong side of outer fabric A. Place the batting on top. Spray again and then top that with the Insul~Brite.

3. Repeat step for both of the outer shell side B pieces.

4. Pin together A and B with right sides together, matching up the dots; then sew.

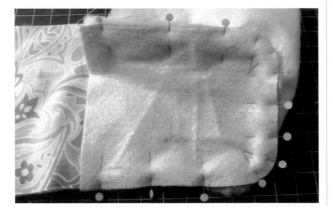

Strap

1. Pin together 2 strap pieces, right sides together.

2. Sew each long edge and trim the seam allowance.

3. Turn the strap right side out.

4. Iron both sides. Topstitch several rows.

5. Pin the strap to one outer shell side B where marked, right sides together. Sew. Then sew a second time to reinforce the straps, making sure to stitch inside the seam allowance.

6. Repeat Step 5 to attach the other end of the strap.

Flap

1. Using quilting basting spray, spray the wrong side of the C piece cut from facing fabric. Place the batting on top. Spray again and then top that with the Insul~Brite.

2. Pin and sew the remaining piece of hook-and-loop tape to the front of the C piece cut from the facing fabric, as indicated on the illustration (page 8).

3. Pin facing C to outer piece C, right sides together. Sew, leaving the straight side open.

4. Notch the corners. Turn inside out and press.

5. Line up the raw edge of the flap with the back of the bag, right sides together. (The flap should line up with the side seams.) Pin and sew, making sure to stitch inside the seam allowance.

Attaching the Lining

1. Trim any excess batting and clip the corners of the outside of the bag. Turn the outer shell right side out.

2. Insert the outer shell into the lining, with right sides together. Line up the edges and pin in place. Sew a ¼″ seam all the way around the top of the bag and both flaps.

3. Turn the bag right side out through the hole left in the lining. Pull out the lining. Turn in the edges of the hole and sew closed.

4. Iron. Topstitch around the top of the bag, if desired.

I graduated from the Art Institute of Boston at Lesley University with a major in photography. After college, I worked in a custom drapery shop, where I acquired skills that I eventually used to open Lucy Blaire Creations, where I am both designer and seamstress. My online Etsy shop is just one of many accomplishments in this new venture. I spend my time running my shop, doing freelance work for other shops and interior designers, and writing books.

www.LucyBlaireCreations.etsy.com

MADE BY
Lucy Blaire

Reusable Lunch Bag and Matching Sandwich Bag

Finished lunch bag size: 7″ × 9″ × 5″

Finished sandwich bag size: 8″ × 8″

The classic design of this double-handled bag lets fabric steal the show. With a coordinating zip-top snack sack, this set is a great choice for those looking for a durable, low-maintenance bag that has timeless appeal.

MATERIALS AND CUTTING INSTRUCTIONS

⅝ yard green oilcloth:

- Cut 2 strips 2″ × 8½″ for sandwich bag binding.
- Cut 1 strip 6″ × 30″ for lunch bag sides.
- Cut 2 pieces 8″ × 10″ for lunch bag front and back.
- Cut 2 strips 2″ × 14″ for lunch bag handles.

¾ yard gingham pattern oilcloth:

- Cut 1 strip 8″ × 18″ for sandwich bag front and back.
- Cut 1 strip 6″ × 30″ for lunch bag lining sides.
- Cut 2 pieces 8″ × 10″ for lunch bag lining front/back.

1 quart-size freezer plastic zipper bag (Use the kind of zipper bag you press together, not the kind with the zipper tab.)

1 yard 1″-wide yellow nylon webbing:

- Cut 2 pieces 14″ each for lunch bag handles.

Walking foot

1 heavy-duty needle

Double-stick tape

CONSTRUCTION

Note: *When working with oilcloth you* **must** *use a walking foot to gently feed the cloth through the machine. Adjust the tension as necessary. Remember to use a fresh needle for each project.*

Assembling the Sandwich Bag

1. Place the 8″ × 18″ gingham oilcloth right side down on a table. Fold in each 8″ end by 1″ and finger-press. Unfold both ends, and fold again at ½″ to make ½″ double folds on each end.

2. Zip shut the closure on the plastic bag. Cut out the "zipper," leaving a ½″ seam allowance above the zipper and a ¼″ seam allowance below it. Pull the pieces apart.

3. Position the top ½″ side of the zipper underneath the open flap of the double fold, making sure there is a space between the zipper and the bottom of the double fold. Stitch on the edge of the double fold to secure the plastic zip in place. Stitch down the other side of the zip, and repeat on the other end with the other half of the zipper.

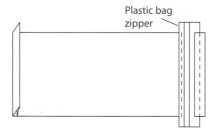

Plastic bag zipper

4. Align the zips and seal, making sure the edges of the bag meet up. Crease the bottom of the bag. Using a ⅛″ seam allowance, stitch down the sides to close the bag.

5. Take a 2″ × 8½″ strip of green oilcloth, fold it in half lengthwise, and finger-press. Unfold and fold each side into the center and finger-press again. Fold in half again so you have a double-folded binding. Repeat with the other green oilcloth strip.

6. Position a piece of the green oilcloth binding just above the top of the sandwich bag, about ⅟₁₆″ above, and use a ¼″ seam allowance to stitch down the bag. Start with multiple backstitches at the top to secure the bag, and then continue down the sides. Before reaching the end, snip off any extra binding at the bottom; then continue sewing, remembering to backstitch a few times at the bottom. Repeat on the other side of the bag.

Preparing the Lunch Bag Pieces

1. Place a piece of 6″ × 30″ gingham oilcloth right side down. Place a few strips of double-stick tape down the center of the wrong side of the oilcloth. Then place the piece of 6″ × 30″ green oilcloth on top, right side up. The tape is used in place of pins to hold the pieces steady. (**Note**: *Do not put the tape near the outer edges of your project, where the needle will go, or else the needle will get sticky.*)

2. Using a ¼″ seam allowance, stitch down the 2 long sides of the fabric. Set aside.

3. Take a 2″ × 17″ strip of green oilcloth and press under ¼″ along one 17″ side. Repeat with the other 2″ × 17″ strip.

4. For this step, you may need to increase the tension on your sewing machine. Place a strip of nylon webbing on your work surface. Place one creased 2″ × 17″ oilcloth strip on top, right side up, so the creased edge aligns with the edge of the nylon webbing. Topstitch down the side, using a ⅛″ seam allowance.

5. Crease the other side of the 2″ × 17″ strip so it lines up with the other edge of the nylon webbing. Topstitch to form a complete covered handle.

6. Repeat Steps 4 and 5 for the other strip of webbing and 2″ × 17″ oilcloth, so you end up with 2 covered handles.

Assembling the Lunch Bag

1. Place an 8″ × 10″ piece of green oilcloth right side up on your work surface. Measure in 1½″ from either side of the 8″ end and mark 2 sections 1″ long . Place the 2 ends of the oilcloth-covered handle, oilcloth side down, in the 1″ sections, with ½″ of the handle overhanging the green oilcloth. Backstitch a few times over both ends of the handle, using a ¼″ seam allowance.

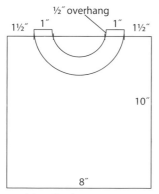

Mark handle placement.

2. Repeat Step 1 with the other 8″ × 10″ piece of green oilcloth and the other handle.

3. Place an 8″ × 10″ piece of gingham oilcloth on top of the "handled" oilcloth, right sides together. Sew together both pieces of oilcloth along the top, using a ¼″ seam allowance.

4. Open the oilcloth so the wrong sides of the cloth are facing and the handles stand up. Crease the seam and top stitch across the top with a ¼″ seam allowance.

5. Repeat Steps 3 and 4 with the other handled piece and the other gingham piece.

6. Place a few pieces of double-stick tape between the 8″ × 10″ pieces. Press together with your fingers. Using a ¼″ seam allowance, stitch together the remaining 3 sides.

7. Place a handled 8″ × 10″ piece green side up on the sewing machine. Place the 6″ × 30″ strip green side down on top, with 1″ hanging over the 8″ × 10″ piece. Start sewing 2″ down from the top of the 8″ × 10″ piece, using a ½″ seam allowance. Continue sewing until you reach ½″ from the bottom corner. Place your needle in the down position and lift the presser foot. Holding the 30″ strip taut with your right hand and the 8″ × 10″ strip steady with your left hand, ease the 30″ strip to the left, folding it as you go. Once the strip is lying flat, turn the entire project to the left 90 degrees. Put the presser foot back down and backstitch the corner twice; then continue sewing. Repeat with the next corner and stitch up the last side, stopping 2″ from the top. There should be at least 1″ overhang on this side as well; if there is more, just trim it down to 1″. (**Note**: *If you aren't used to doing this type of corner, you can also use the lines of the gingham pattern as a guide. Stop sewing on a line, even if it is not exactly ½″ from the bottom. This way, when you need to match up the corners, you can just go by the lines of the gingham.*)

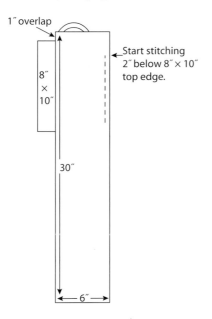

1″ overlap

8″
×
10″

Start stitching
2″ below 8″ × 10″
top edge.

30″

6″

8. Place the second handled 8″ × 10″ piece green side up on the sewing machine. Place the piece you just sewed in Step 7 on top, so the 8″ × 10″ pieces line up. Sew the other side of the 30″ strip to the 8″ × 10″ piece. Remember to begin and end your stitching 2″ from the top of the bag.

9. Open the bag and stand it upright, so the 5″ side faces you. Use a seam ripper to separate the 2 side layers of the oilcloth down to where you began your stitching, 2″ from the top. Fold down the green oilcloth and crease it to align with the two 8″ × 10″ pieces. Flip the bag over onto your sewing machine and fold the gingham oilcloth inside to align with the green oilcloth. Using a ¼″ seam allowance, top stitch across the top. Repeat with the other side. Stitch up the 2″ gap so the entire 30″ strip is attached to the 8″ × 10″ pieces.

10. Trim the side and bottom seams to a bit less than ¼″. Turn the bag right side out and flatten and crease all the seams to form a clean box shape.

11. Topstitch both sides and the bottom of each 8″ × 10″ piece. Backstitch multiple times at the top, sew down the side, and backstitch again. Start each seam fresh with backstitches at both the top and bottom of each side. These finishing seams act to both hide the inside seams and give the bag added strength.

I first started making these lunch bags when my mom complained that the commercial ones weren't big enough to hold both her potato chips and her water bottle without crushing the chips. I made a bag for her that was taller than usual but that could easily be squashed down for a smaller lunch. Most of what I create is practical yet imaginative. Often my inspiration is something that I wish I had but can't find. My pup and I live and work in Pennsylvania.

www.NeedfulThingsofSalem.etsy.com

MADE BY
Leslie Bowman

Piggy Lunch Bag

Finished size: 6″ × 9¾″ × 4″

In his denim overalls, this pig makes the perfect companion for the younger crowd. A perfectly proportioned handle and an insulated interior are sensible touches but the appliqué and embroidered face are pure whimsy.

MATERIALS

⅝ yard main color fabric

⅝ yard fusible batting

⅝ yard lining fabric (e.g., muslin)

⅓ yard tearaway stabilizer

⅓ yard contrasting colored fabric for overalls

¼ yard very stiff interfacing

1 square pink felt (or to match main color fabric)

Scraps of white felt

Black, white, and gold fabric paints

CONSTRUCTION

Patterns can be found on pages 120-122.

1. Rather than make a pattern piece for the bag itself, I mark off a 21″ × 10¾″ rectangle. Then I place the larger U-shaped template (page 121) ½″ from one edge and trace. Cut 1 template from the main fabric, 1 from the fusible batting, and 1 from the lining fabric. Trim the interfacing ½″ from each short side and from the bottom, then trim ¼″ from the upper edge.

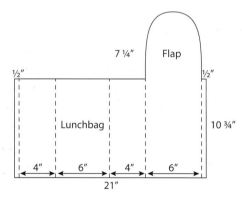

Lunch bag template

2. Fuse the batting to the back of the main fabric. Using the flap template (page 121), cut a U-shaped piece of the very stiff interfacing. Trim ¼″ off the curved edge. Align it along the seam allowance and baste to the inside of the interfacing/main fabric piece. Pin the lining fabric to the main fabric with right sides together. Sew along the top edge including the flap. Trim, turn, and press. Topstitch if desired.

3. With wrong sides together, sew along the dashed lines shown on the lunch bag template illustration (left) to mark the edges of the bag (but not at the ½″ seamlines on the edges). Serge the lower edge or simply stitch the lower edges together.

4. Cut out the overalls using the front and back templates (page 120). Using tracing paper or a lightbox and light tracer, mark the overalls fabric along the dashed lines (shown on the pattern), so you'll know where to place the contrast stitches. Secure tearaway stabilizer to the wrong side of the overalls fabric.

5. Position the overalls ¾″ above the bottom edge of the main fabric. Attach the overalls to the main fabric by sewing along the solid lines/outer edges, using matching colored thread and a short zigzag stitch. Use contrasting thread to topstitch along the dashed lines.

6. Cut 4 arms (page 122) from the pink felt. Sew together 2 arm pieces, close to the edge. Repeat with the remaining 2 arm pieces. Sew the arms to the sides of the bag wherever you like.

7. With right sides together, sew the side seam, using a ½″ seam allowance; then serge, pink, or zigzag stitch the seam allowance.

8. For the bottom of the bag, cut a 5″ × 7″ piece of the main color fabric and a 5″ × 7″ piece of the lining fabric. Cut a 4″ × 6″ piece of fusible interfacing and a 4″ × 6″ piece of stiff interfacing. Center the fusible interfacing and fuse it to the wrong side of the main fabric. Baste the stiff interfacing in place on top of the fusible interfacing. Place the lining fabric on top of the interfacing.

Baste and then stitch close to the interfacing. With right sides facing, pin this to the bag, matching corners and corner seams. Stitch, using a ½″ seam allowance.

9. Sew a small piece of hook-and-loop tape on the flap lining and then sew its mate approximately 2½″ from the top center edge of the bag front.

10. Cut 4 ear pieces from the pink felt. Sew pairs together, close to the edge and along the dashed lines. Attach the ears to the bag by stitching close to the edge and along the dashed lines.

11. Cut 2 eyes from white felt. Paint the edges and pupils with black fabric paint, as indicated on the pattern. Allow paint to dry before adding the white highlight.

12. Cut a nose from the pink felt. Paint the edge and nostrils with black fabric paint. Allow to dry. Center the nose over the hook-and-loop tape seam and sew along the edge. Place the eyes where desired and sew by machine or by hand. Paint a smile on the piggy. Use gold paint or French knots for buttons on the overalls.

13. For the handle, cut a 16″ × 3″ strip of contrast fabric. Cut a 15″ × 1″ (or slightly narrower) strip of fusible interfacing. Turn under a ½″ seam allowance along the long edges of the contrast fabric. Fuse the interfacing, aligning one edge with the fabric's folded edge. Fold in half. Topstitch both long edges of the handle using contrasting thread. Turn under ½″ of each short edge to the inside and stitch. Center the handle's edges along the top edge of the bag's side panels. Sew an X-in-box pattern to secure.

W orking in downtown Baltimore, I noticed that many women on their way to work carried expensive, fashionable purses, but their lunch bags did not express the same fashion sense. After trial and error, I created the lunch purse to give some added style to women who carry their lunch to work.

The Pattypan Shop is the creation of three daughters working with their moms to provide cute and "carryable" items that are unique and innovative. With four sewers and one yarn artisan, the shop offers a variety of products for just about anyone with a classic, unique sense of style. The most popular item has been my lunch purses.

www.thepattypanshop.etsy.com

MADE BY
Denise Clark

Executive Insulated Lunch Purse

Finished size: 10″ × 8½″ × 5½″

This stylish bag belies its practical construction. The extra long zipper allows the top to open exposing a fully-lined interior. A durable canvas bottom and straps ensure a chic, enduring solution for an eco-conscious fashionista.

MATERIALS AND CUTTING INSTRUCTIONS

½ yard medium-weight or home decor cotton fabric for front, back, and zipper ends:

- Cut 2 pattern As for purse front and back.
- Cut 2 pieces 2″ × 3″ for zipper ends.

⅓ yard cotton duck for purse bottom and straps:

- Cut 2 pattern Bs for purse bottom.
- Cut 2 pieces 4″ × 15″ for straps.

½ yard medium-weight fusible interfacing for front and back:

- Cut 2 pattern As for front and back.
- Cut 2 pieces 4″ × 15″ for straps (optional).

½ yard cotton fabric for lining:

- Cut 1 pattern C (on fold) for lining.

½ yard insulating material (e.g., Insul~Brite) for insulation:

- Cut 1 pattern C (on fold) for insulation.

18″ zipper

Water-soluble fabric marker

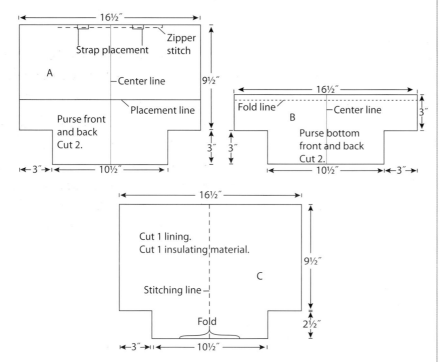

CONSTRUCTION

Note: *All seam allowances are ½″ unless otherwise indicated. Mark all pieces as indicated.*

Assembling the Purse

1. Turn under the top of the B pieces ½″ and press.

2. Align the bottom pieces (B) with the placement lines marked on the right sides of the front and back pieces (A). Pin in place and topstitch.

3. Follow the manufacturer's instructions to apply fusible interfacing to the wrong sides of the front and back pieces (A) and to the wrong sides of the straps (optional). Trim any excess interfacing from around the edges.

Attaching the Straps

1. Fold the straps in half lengthwise, wrong sides together, and press. Open the straps and fold the lengthwise edges toward the center line created by the fold. Press the edges in place. Bring the folded edges together. Stitch close to the edge along both lengthwise edges of each strap.

2. Pin the straps to the front and back pieces, as indicated on pattern A. Make sure that the front and back straps are in alignment and that there are no twists in the straps. Stitch the straps ⅛″ in from the top.

Installing the Zipper

1. Trim off approximately ½″ from each end of the 18″ zipper.

2. Press down a ¼″ of one short end of the fabric zipper tab. Then press down ¼″ of both long ends. Then press down the remaining short end. Fold in half. Slip the zipper between the folded fabric zipper tabs and stitch around all sides. Repeat for the other end of the zipper. Refer to the photo on page 73, though the zipper ends will extend out further for this project.

3. With the wrong side of the zipper showing, mark its center by folding it in half. Place fabric A (front) and the zipper right sides together, aligning the zipper's center mark with the center mark of piece A (front). Mark the zipper 4¾″ on either side of the center mark. Pin the zipper in place; then stitch it in place 9½″ between the marks. There will be excess zipper at each end.

4. Repeat Step 3 with fabric A (back) and ensure that the straps are aligned with the straps on the front.

Sewing the Sides, Bottom, and Corner Seams

1. Place the front and back pieces right sides together. Stitch together the sides and bottom of the bag. Make sure the zipper remains free.

2. Referring to the Corner Construction Techniques (pages 118–119), stitch the corners on each side of the bag. Turn the bag right side out. Press the top edge down ½″.

Lining and Insulating the Bag

1. Align the lining and insulating material C wrong sides together and pin in place. Stitch the pieces together as indicated on the pattern C stitching lines. Press down ½″ at the top.

2. Fold with right sides together and stitch the front and back lining to the insulating fabric along the sides. Then stitch the corners on each side of the lining through all the layers (as with the outer fabric).

FINISHING

1. Insert the lining into the bag. Fold the top of the lining under ½″, and pin it in place. Stitch the lining to the bag along the top edge through all the layers.

2. Pinch each corner of the bag ⅛″ from where the zipper stitches end. Pin in place. Zip the bag closed to make sure the corners (front and back) are aligned. Then topstitch ⅛″ from the edge of the bag about 1″ long from the top. (**Note:** *A nice sharp needle will be your best friend because of the thickness.*) Neatly trim any excess threads.

I am a Kansas girl who has always loved art and—yes—craft! Influenced particularly by Victorian and prairie fashions, the circus, and ethnic folk costumes, I began designing my own unique fashions. From my Etsy store, I sell one-of-a-kind clothing and accessories that are romantic and whimsical, but also chic and modern. My other pursuits include knitting, gardening, and supporting handmade and local businesses.

www.folk.etsy.com

www.folkcraft.blogspot.com

MADE BY
Leanne Dougherty

Mushroom Picnic Bag

Finished size: 9″ × 10″ × 5″

Sophisticated and fun, this trendy bag is embellished with decorative lace and a vintage button closure and embroidered with a handsome group of mushrooms. Classic linen combines with a soft blue cotton ticking lining to create a bag that's full of class.

MATERIALS AND CUTTING INSTRUCTIONS

½ yard linen for outer fabric:

- Cut 2 rectangles 12½″ × 15″.

½ yard striped ticking (or any sturdy, canvaslike material) for lining:

- Cut 2 rectangles 12½″ × 15″.

6″ length of cord or elastic for loop closure

¾ yard 3¼″-wide lace

¾ yard 2¼″-wide lace

1 large button

Embroidery floss

PREPARING THE FABRIC

1. Take one piece of linen. From the corner of each shorter 12½″ side, cut a 2½″ × 2½″ square notch, so that the piece is in the shape of a very thick T. Repeat this step with the other piece of linen and the lining fabric.

2. Cut each piece of lace in half. On the right side of the linen, position the narrower lace across the width, so that it sits 1″ above the corner notches. Pin in place and topstitch to secure. Layer the wide lace on top of the stitched-on lace; pin and topstitch along both edges. Repeat with the other piece of linen.

3. Use the mushroom template (page 123) or create your own original design. Transfer your chosen design to the right side of the linen. Center the design along the 12½″ edge of the linen so that the bottom of the design is approximately ¾″ from the top edge of the fabric. (**Note**: *If the piece of fabric is lying in front of you so that the notches and lace are toward the bottom and the embroidery design is at the top, the design should be upside down. In this way, when the flap is turned down, the design will appear upright.*) Use a straight stitch to hand or machine embroider your design. I used French knots for the mushroom dots.

4. Position the raw ends of the loop (cord or elastic) on the top edge of the right side of the linen, right next to the embroidered design. The loop should be centered, with the ends approximately 2½″–3″ apart. Pin and baste in place.

CONSTRUCTION

1. Place a linen piece on a ticking piece, right sides together. Pin along the top. Stitch across the top, using a ½″ seam allowance. Repeat with the other side.

2. Open up both of the pieces you just stitched together. With right sides together, match ticking to ticking and linen to linen. Pin all around. Stitch around all sides except for a 6″ gap at the center of the bottom of the ticking—this will be left open to turn later. Do not stitch the edges of the square notches yet.

3. To create the "square" bottom, to give the bag dimension, and to allow it to stand on its own, you must now sew the notches. To do this, open a notch. Then press it together in the opposite direction of how it would naturally lie, creasing it at the corners so that the side seam and the bottom seams are all aligned. Pin and stitch across the corner. Repeat for each corner. Refer to Corner Construction Techniques on pages 118–119.

4. Reach into the open seam at the bottom and turn the bag inside out. To close the hole after it is turned, pin the seam together and topstitch with the sewing machine; or for a more finished look, hand stitch using a ladder stitch. Stuff the ticking back into the linen and press the seams. Fold down the flap so the embroidered design is showing, and attach the button so that the loop can reach it. (Placement of the button will depend on the size of your button and how much you want to fold the top down.)

I've always had an affinity for anything handmade, and I've enjoyed needlecrafts all my life. After friends and relatives started requesting handmade gifts, I realized that many others also shared my love for such items, and this led to my becoming a professional dollmaker. Now I like to mix things up and work on other arts, but I always find myself coming back to fibers. My focus is on quilting, totes, and accessories, using the gorgeous designer fabrics on the market. Making eco-friendly, reusable, useful items from these beautiful fabrics is something that gives me great pleasure.

MADE BY
Jane Fitzpatrick

www.solsticestudio.etsy.com

Eco-Friendly Lunch Bag

Finished size: 8″ × 10″ × 3½″

Let the fabric lead the way with this quintessential design. With the addition of a handle and a button-closure top, the standard sack gets a significant upgrade.

MATERIALS AND CUTTING INSTRUCTIONS

⅝ yard fabric for outer bag and handle:

- Cut 1 piece 12″ × 19″ for back/flap.*
- Cut 1 piece 12″ × 13″ for front.
- Cut 1 piece 4″ × 13″ for handle.

⅝ yard fabric for lining and inner pocket:

- Cut 1 piece 12″ × 19″ for back/flap.*
- Cut 1 piece 12″ × 13″ for front.
- Cut 2 pieces 3½″ × 6″ for pocket.

- Cut 2 pieces 3½″ × 8½″ for sleeve to cover plastic canvas (optional).

½ yard fusible fleece:

- Cut 1 piece 12″ × 19″ for back/flap.*
- Cut 1 piece 12″ × 13″ for front.
- Cut 1 piece 1″ × 13″ for handle.

7″ length of cording for loop closure

1¼″–1½″-wide button

3″ × 8″ plastic canvas for bottom (optional)

* To cut the back/flap shape, stack the 12″ × 19″ pieces for the outer bag, lining, and interfacing. Measure across 1¾″ from each side and 6″ down from the top, as shown. It's easier to cut all 3 pieces at once.

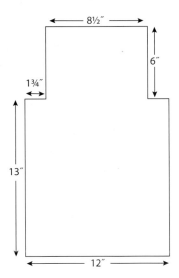

CONSTRUCTION

Note: *All seam allowances are ⅜″.*

Assembling the Bag

1. Fuse or baste the fleece to the wrong side of the outer back/flap piece and the outer front piece.

2. To make the button loop, fold the cording in half. Place the cording on the right side of the flap, with the ends of the cording extending ⅛″ past the raw edge of the flap. Make sure the cording is centered. Stitch across the cording close to the edge of the flap.

3. Sew the outer front to the outer back/flap, right sides together and aligning the bottom edges. Sew along the sides and the bottom.

4. To form the bottom box corners, refold the bag, right sides together, aligning the side seam with the bottom seam on one side of the bag. Stitch perpendicular to the seamline about 1½″ from the point. Trim off the corner ¼″ outside the stitching. Repeat for the other side. Turn the bag right side out.

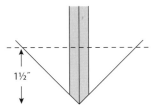

5. To make the handle, fold the fabric in half lengthwise, wrong sides together, and press. Open this crease and fold the raw edges into the center crease. Press. Open the fold on one side and sandwich the fleece next to the crease. Refold and topstitch through all the layers along both long sides, close to the edge.

6. Center the handle end on the right side of one of the bag's side seams, with raw edges even. Sew across the handle, close to the edge. Repeat for the other side, being careful not to twist the handle. Set aside.

7. For the lining pocket, sew the pocket pieces right sides together along the sides and the top. Turn and press. Tuck in the raw edges of the pocket bottom. Place the pocket on the right side of the lining back/ flap piece, 3½˝ up from the bottom and centered. Stitch close to the edge around the sides and bottom of the pocket.

8. Sew the lining pieces together as you did for the outer bag (Step 3). Leave a 5˝ opening across the center bottom of the lining (to turn the bag later). Make the box corners as you did with the outer bag in Step 4.

9. Insert the outer bag into the lining, aligning the side seams and flaps, with all pieces right sides together. It is helpful to use a safety pin to hold the handle and loop closure in place. Pin together and sew around the front and the flap, reinforcing the stitches at the inner corners near the flap. Make a few snips into the corners so the bag will lie flat when turned.

10. To turn, pull the bag out through the opening in the lining bottom. Pull up the flap. Use the opening in the lining to push up the flap and poke the corners out a bit. Tuck the lining into the outer bag. Once the bag is completely turned, fold in the raw edges along the lining bottom and stitch closed. Topstitch all around the top edge and the flap.

FINISHING

1. Sew the button on the front so it falls in the middle of the loop when the flap is closed.

2. To give the bag more structure, insert a fabric covered piece of plastic canvas inside the bottom of the bag. To do so, place the 2 fabric sleeve pieces right sides together and stitch around both long sides and one short side using a ¼˝ seam allowance. Turn and press. Insert the plastic canvas into the sleeve. Tuck in the raw edges and slipstitch the open side closed. Insert ito the bag bottom.

I was born and raised in San Jose, California, and consider myself the third generation of very creative individuals who always encouraged a passion for learning and creating art. My grandmother taught me to crochet at the age of eight. In 2007, I started selling my crochet goods online. Largely influenced by the simplicity and vibrating colors of the 60s and 70s, today my handmade creations mostly consist of crocheted wearables/usables and kitschy hair accessories.

I live in the beautiful mountains of Asheville, North Carolina, with my equally creative and supportive husband and our three children.

www.earlygirl.etsy.com

www.flickr.com/people/earlygrrrl

MADE BY
Shannon Fowler-Wardrep

Apple-A-Go-Go

Finished size: 4″ × 4″ × 4″

Protect your fruit from bumps and bruises with a crocheted cozy. If you are new to crochet, this achievable project will have you hooked. Add a vintage button for a fun project that is sure to attract attention.

MATERIALS AND SUPPLIES

Yarn (1 or 2 colors)

Button

Tapestry needle

E/4 (3.5mm) hook

Stitch marker

CONSTRUCTION

ch – chain   sl st – slip stitch

sts – stitches   sc – single crochet

To begin: Chain 4; form a ring by making 1 sl st into 1st ch.

Round 1: Work 6 sc in a ring.

Round 2: sc 2 in each sc around—12 sts.

Round 3: *sc in next sc, sc 2 in next sc; repeat from * around 6 times—18 sts.

Round 4: *sc in next 2 sc, sc 2 in next sc; repeat from * around 6 times—24 sts.

Round 5: *sc in next 3 sc, sc 2 in next sc; repeat from * around 6 times—30 sts.

Rounds 6–8: *sc in next and each sc around; repeat from * around 3 times—30 sts for each round.

Forming the V Opening

Round 9: ch 1, turn, sc 2 in 1st sc, sc in next sc around, sc 2 in last sc—32 sts.

Round 10: ch 1, turn, sc 2 in 1st sc, sc in next sc around, sc 2 in last sc—34 sts.

Rounds 11–17: ch 1, turn, sc in each sc around—34 sts.

Incorporate a second yarn color at the beginning of row 15 (optional).

Round 18: ch 1, turn, *sc in 1 sc, sl st 2 sc together; repeat from *, sc 1 in last sc—23 sts.

Crocheting the Edge of the V Opening

Going down the right side: sc 3 in next sc, *skip 1 sc, sc 2 in next sc, repeat from *—13 sts.

Center of V: sc 1 in each sc—2 sts.

Going up the left side: *sc 2 in next sc, skip 1 sc, repeat from *—10 sts.

Do not turn.

Round 19: *sc 3 in 1 sc, sl st 2 sc together; repeat from *, sc 1 in last sc—15 sts.

To form loop: sl st in next 2 sc, ch 12, sl st in same st, sl st in next st.

FINISHING

Cut off, leaving a long enough tail of yarn to pull back through to the inside of the apple sweater. Weave in the end at the base of the loop to reinforce. With the same color yarn, sew a button on the opposite side of the apple sweater. Weave in the ends. Finished size fits a small to medium apple.

dirtsa is the creation of mother-and-daughter team Karen and Rebecca Garcia. We began creating custom textile goods as an outgrowth of our love of fabric, colors, and patterns. Mom Karen has many years of sewing experience, creating apparel and home decorating projects and teaching students to create their own beautiful quilts and handiwork. She is a top-notch cook, loves to read, and dabbles in many crafts, including basketry, beading, and stenciling, to name just a few.

Rebecca loves form and design in addition to color and pattern. She studied American arts and material at Yale University and earned a master's degree in American decorative arts at the Winterthur Museum. Her studies have informed both her personal and professional creative designs, which can be viewed at RebeccaJGarcia.com.

www.shopdirtsa.com
www.dirtsa.etsy.com

MADE BY
Rebecca and Karen Garcia

Insulated Lunch Tote

Finished size: 9″ × 9½″ × 4″

Big enough to hold a drink and reusable container but small enough for kids to take to school, the basic shape features hook-and-loop tape, resilient canvas handles, and a practical removable vinyl insert that makes for quick cleanup of the messier lunches.

MATERIALS AND CUTTING INSTRUCTIONS

½ yard exterior fabric (*Home decor fabric, canvas, or duck cloth are recommended fabric weights.*)

- Cut 1 rectangle 15″ × 24″.
- Cut 2 rectangles 5½″ × 10½″.

½ yard lining fabric:

- Cut 1 rectangle 15″ × 24″.

½ yard Insul~Brite (thermal lining):

- Cut 1 rectangle 15″x 24″.

⅓ yard sew-on hook-and-loop tape:

- Cut 2 lengths 5½″ each.

1¾ yards 1″-wide webbing for handles and flap:

- Cut 2 lengths 27″ each for handles.
- Cut 1 length 3½″ for flap pull.

⅓ yard clear vinyl:

- Cut 1 piece 9″ × 25½″.
- Cut 1 piece 9″ × 4″.

CONSTRUCTION

Note: *Seam allowances are ½″ unless otherwise noted.*

Assembling the Flap

1. To make the angles on the flap, place the 5½″ × 10½″ rectangles on top of each other, right sides together. Along one long side, mark 2½″ in from each corner in both directions. Draw a diagonal line connecting the marks to form a triangle. Cut along the drawn line.

2. On the right side of a flap piece, position a hook piece of hook-and-loop tape along the long angled edge, approximately ¾″ from the edge and centered from left to right. Stitch in place. Stitch the other hook piece next to the first to form a wide hook-and-loop tape rectangle (see photo on page 41).

3. To create the flap pull, make a loop with the 3½″ piece of webbing by bringing the cut edges together. Center the loop over the hook-and-loop tape, with the loop facing into the flap and the cut edges of the webbing even with the edge of the flap. Stitch close to the raw edges to hold in place.

4. Pin the 2 flap pieces right sides together (the loop and hook-and-loop tape will be sandwiched in the middle). Stitch around the perimeter, *leaving the straight 10½″ side open.*

5. Trim the corner seam allowances and turn the flap right side out, being sure to push out the corners. Press.

6. Topstitch ¼″ around the edges of the flap.

Assembling the Bag

1. With the 15″ × 24″ exterior fabric facing right side up, center the open edges of the flap along a 15″ edge, *making sure the hook-and-loop tape side is facing up.* Stitch in place along the edge. The side with the flap will become the back of the bag.

2. Place the lining fabric on top of the exterior fabric, right sides together (the flap will be sandwiched in between). Place the Insul~Brite on top of the lining fabric, with the shiny side facing up. Pin the 3 layers together.

3. Stitch around all the edges, *leaving a 6″ opening in the middle of one of the 24″ sides.* To reduce bulk, trim the corners and trim away the Insul~Brite seam allowance close to the stitching.

4. Turn the bag right side out, making sure to push out the corners. Turn in the seam allowance along the opening and stitch closed. Topstitch the short sides of the rectangle (i.e., the top edges of the bag).

5. Center the remaining lengths of hook-and-loop tape on the short edge opposite the flap. Pin the first piece of hook-and-loop tape 2¼″ down from the top edge of the exterior fabric. Stitch in place through all 3 layers. Stitch the remaining piece of hook-and-loop tape directly below the first.

Attaching the Handles

1. To prevent unraveling, use a zigzag stitch along the cut edges of the webbing, or apply Dritz Fray Check.

2. The handles are placed along the short sides of the bag rectangle. Choose a short side of this rectangle; measure and mark 3″ in from both corners (A). Then measure and mark 4″ down from mark A (B). Align the outside edges of a length of webbing with the A marks and the cut edges with the B marks. Pin in place, making sure the loop of webbing is not twisted.

3. Attach the handles securely by stitching a 1″ × 1″ square at each end of the webbing (near B). Stitch an X inside the square for extra reinforcement.

4. Repeat with the remaining webbing on the opposite side of the bag.

FINISHING

1. Fold the bag rectangle in half widthwise, right sides together, aligning the top edges. Pin the side edges together.

2. Sew the side edges together. A ¼″–⅜″ seam allowance works well for this seam.

3. To form a flat bottom, place your hand in the bag with your index finger poking into the corner. With the thumb and index finger of your other hand, pinch the corner down and away from the bag. The bottom of the bag will flatten out. Consider the corner of the bag to be the tip of a triangle. From the tip of the triangle, measure about 2″ along the side seam to establish the base of the triangle. This base is perpendicular to the side seam. Mark this baseline (approximately 4″ long), with the side seam at the center of the line. Stitch along the marked baseline. Repeat on the other side of the bag. Refer to Corner Construction Techniques on pages 118–119.

4. Turn the bag right side out and push the triangles down to provide support for the bottom of the bag.

5. *Optional:* Form structured sides on the bag by creasing the bag lengthwise about 2″ on both sides of each side seam. Stitch close to the folded edge to hold the crease in place.

Vinyl Liner

Tips for sewing with vinyl:

Needle holes made in vinyl are permanent, and too many perforations make vinyl easy to tear. To minimize the number of needle holes, follow these suggestions:

Use a slightly longer stitch length.

Do not backstitch at the end of a seam; instead, apply a dab of Fray Check or glue to the ends of the thread.

Use paper clips rather than pins to hold pieces together.

Vinyl tends to stick to the bottom of metal presser feet on sewing machines, which prevents the vinyl from being pulled forward through the machine. Many sewing machines come equipped with a Teflon presser foot to use with vinyl and leather. If you do not have this accessory, there is no need to purchase one. Instead, apply a piece of regular clear tape across the bottom of your metal presser foot and use scissors to trim the tape to fit. The presser foot will now glide over the vinyl.

1. The small piece of vinyl is the bottom of the liner. The long piece of vinyl is attached to the edges of the bottom to create the 4 sides. Start by lining up a corner of the small piece with a corner of the large piece, along the long edge. Begin stitching ½" from the corner. Stop ½" from the next corner and make a small clip (¼"–½") in the large piece of vinyl. The cut will provide the ease necessary to turn the vinyl around the corner. Proceed in the same way along the other sides, ending ½" before the first corner.

2. Line up the 2 lengthwise edges and stitch with a ½" seam.

3. Insert the vinyl liner into the lunch bag.

I am the designer behind Unspeakable Visions, a small-scale, home-based studio that encourages the enjoyment of simple pleasures through handmade goods. The collections are thoughtful, deliberate, and limited. Each item is made with quality materials and careful craftsmanship to create a lasting heirloom. From pure linen tea towels with original block-printed designs to reusable cotton lunch bags and quilted coasters, the goods are a celebration of a simpler, more meaningful appreciation for handmade craft.

www.unspeakablevisions.com

MADE BY
Christine Hmiel

Simple Lunch Bag

Finished size: 8½" × 12½" × 5"

Sweet and simple, this lunch bag can go from stylish to kid-friendly depending on the fabric. A handy pocket and roll-over top take the traditional sack shape to the next level. The quick construction makes this the perfect bag for gifting or personalizing for every member of the family.

MATERIALS AND CUTTING INSTRUCTIONS

¾ yard heavyweight cotton fabric for lunch bag and pocket:

- Cut 1 main panel 30" × 14½".
- Cut 1 pocket panel 4½" × 5½".

1 yard contrasting double-fold bias tape for lunch bag and pocket trim:

- Cut 1 strip 28" in length for main panel trim.
- Cut 1 strip 5½" in length for pocket panel trim.

Sew-on hook-and-loop tape:

- Cut 1 piece 2" in length for lunch bag closure.

Water-soluble fabric marker or fabric pencil

CONSTRUCTION

Note: *All seam allowances are ½" unless otherwise noted.*

1. Make the pin tucks. On the *right* side of the main panel, measure and mark 3" in all the way down from one long side of the main panel (see illustration at right). Connect the marks to draw a line 3" in from the raw side edge of the panel. Fold on the 3" line with wrong sides together, and press. Topstitch ⅛" from the folded edge, backstitching at both ends. Repeat on the other side of the main panel.

2. Make the pocket. Attach the 5½" strip of bias tape to a long edge of the pocket panel, following the manufacturer's instructions and backstitching at both ends. Then fold under ½" on the short sides and the bottom of the pocket panel; press.

3. Attach the pocket to the main panel. With the *right* side of the main panel facing up, place the pocket panel *wrong* side down so that the top edge is 6" below the top of the main panel and centered horizontally between the pin tucks. Pin in place. Beginning at the top left corner, edgestitch down the pocket side, across the bottom edge, and up the right side, pivoting at the bottom corners and backstitching at both ends.

4. Construct the bag. With *right* sides together, match the short edges of the main panel and then fold the main panel in half. Pin in place. Stitch the raw sides together, backstitching at both ends. Press open the seams. (**Note**: *Use pinking shears or a zigzag stitch to finish the seams.*)

5. Make the gussets. With the wrong side still facing out, measure up 3" from the bottom folded edge along the pin tuck. Using a fabric marker or pencil, mark this spot with a small dot. Draw a line from the dot to the bottom corner of the main panel. Repeat on the right side of the bag.

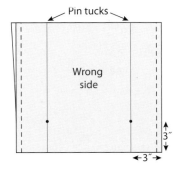

With a side seam facing you, pinch the fabric on the left side of the seam and fold the fabric, *right* sides together, directly on the line you just drew in Step 5. Pin in place. Repeat on the right side of the seam, creating a triangle-shaped gusset. Pin in place.

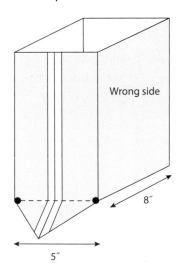

Complete the triangle shape by stitching a straight line to connect the dot on the left side of the seam with the dot on the right side of the seam. Backstitch at both ends.

Repeat the entire process on the other side seam of the bag. The base of your lunch bag should now measure approximately 5″ × 8½″. Using scissors, trim the triangle shape to create a ½″ seam allowance on each gusset.

6. Finish the top raw edge. Turn the bag *right* side out. Attach the 28″ strip of bias tape to the top raw edge, following the manufacturer's instructions.

7. Attach the hook-and-loop tape. Center the rough (hook) piece of hook-and-loop tape horizontally on the front of the lunch bag, 3½″ from the top edge, and pin in place. Stitch close to the edges of the hook-and-loop tape to attach it securely to the bag.

Center the smooth (loop) piece of hook-and-loop tape horizontally on the back of the lunch bag, directly below the bias tape, and pin in place. Stitch close to the edges of the hook-and-loop tape to attach it securely to the bag.

I have been sewing and crafting for as long as I can remember. As a designer, I find it very satisfying to visualize a style and to figure out the mechanics of putting it all together. With each iteration of a design, I learn more about the structure of bags. Often, inspiration comes from the beautiful fabrics available today. Other times, the challenge is trying to find the fabric to complement the design I envision.

www.DWhynnDesigns.etsy.com

www.baggingit.typepad.com

MADE BY
Debbie Hogan

Insulated Lunch Bag with Drink Pouch

Finished size: 7″ × 10″ × 3½″

Innovative and imaginative., this bag has it all: a toggle-cinch drink pocket on the outside, an ingenious looped closure to keep the contents secure, and a slim interior pocket perfect for sliding in an ice pack—all combined with a bias-tape edging adding a finishing touch.

MATERIALS AND CUTTING INSTRUCTIONS

Allow extra yardage for one-way designs.

⅝ yard* fabric for top half of outer bag, flap, and drink pouch:

- Cut 2 rectangles 13½″ × 9½″ for front and back.
- Cut 1 square 9½″ × 9½″ for flap.
- Cut 1 rectangle 12″ × 10″ for drink pouch.

½ yard* fabric for bottom half of outer bag, closure strap, and handle:

- Cut 2 rectangles 13½″ × 6½″ for front and back.
- Cut 1 rectangle 3″ × 21″ for closure strap.
- Cut 1 rectangle 5″ × 16″ for handle.
- Cut 2 rectangles 7″ × 8½″ for inner pocket.

⅝ yard fabric for lining:

- Cut 1 square 9½″ × 9½″ for flap lining.
- Cut 2 rectangles 12″ × 12½″ for bag lining.
- Cut 1 rectangle 11″ × 9″ for drink pouch.
- Cut 1 rectangle 3″ × 11″ for drink pouch casing.

1 fat quarter for bias flap trim and inner pocket:

- Cut 1 strip on the bias 23″ × 2¼″ for flap bias binding.
- Cut 1 rectangle (not on the bias) 8½″ × 2¼″ for inner pocket binding.

⅝ yard 45″-wide insulated batting:

- Cut 2 rectangles 13½″ × 9½″ for front and back top.
- Cut 2 rectangles 13½″ × 6½″ for front and back bottom.
- Cut 1 rectangle 12″ × 10″ for drink pouch.

10″ × 10″ piece thin batting (Do not use insulated batting.)

- Cut 1 square 9½″ × 9½″ for flap.

⅓ yard lightweight fusible interfacing for handle and drink pouch casing:

- Cut 1 rectangle 5″ × 16″ for handle.
- Cut 1 rectangle 3″ × 11″ for drink pouch casing.

2 small grommets (optional)

Thin cording for drink pouch drawstring:

- Cut 2 pieces 11″ each.

1 cord lock

CONSTRUCTION

Note: *All seam allowances are ½″ unless otherwise noted.*

Preparing the Fabrics for the Top and Bottom Half of the Outer Bag

1. Adhere the top and bottom fabric pieces to a layer of insulated batting using your favorite method, such as spray adhesive or pinning; quilt as desired.

2. Cut the quilted fabric pieces to the following final measurements: *Top*: Cut 2 pieces 12″ × 8½″. *Bottom*: Cut 2 pieces 12″ × 5½″.

3. Cut a 2″ × 2″ square notch from each side of the lower corners of the bottom fabrics.

Preparing the Fabrics for the Drink Pouch

1. Adhere the drink pouch fabric to insulated batting and quilt as desired.

2. Cut the drink pouch to a final measurement of 11″ × 9″.

Preparing the Fabrics for the Flap

1. Layer a quilt sandwich consisting of the front flap lining fabric, thin batting, and the front flap fabric; quilt as desired.

2. Cut the quilted fabric to a final measurement of 8½″ × 8½″.

3. Use a can or saucer as a template to round the lower corners of the flap; mark and cut the corners.

Attaching Bias Binding to the Front Flap

1. With wrong sides together, fold the bias strip in half and press.

2. Using a ¼″ seam allowance, sew the bias binding to the edge of the front flap, easing the binding along the lower curved edges.

3. Press the binding to the lining side of the flap and sew the finished edge of the binding by machine or hand stitching.

Making the Closure Strap and Handle

1. Fuse lightweight interfacing to the wrong side of the handle. Do not use interfacing on the closure strap.

2. With wrong sides together, fold the closure strap fabric in half and press. Open the fabric. Repeat with the handle fabric.

3. Fold each long edge to the middle crease line and press.

4. Fold the strip in half lengthwise, enclosing all raw edges. Press.

5. Topstitch down each long side of the strap and handle.

Attaching the Closure Strap and Handle to the Bag

1. Trim the closure strap to a final length of 19½″. Fold in half lengthwise.

2. With raw edges together, stitch the folded strap to the center point of the 12″ edge of one of the bottom pieces. This is now the *front* bottom piece.

3. Trim the handle to a final length of 15″. Fold in half lengthwise.

4. With raw edges together, stitch the folded handled at the center point of the 12″ edge of one of the top pieces. This is now the *back* top piece.

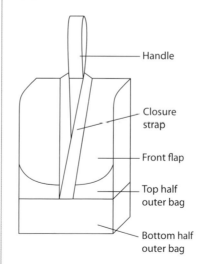

Handle

Closure strap

Front flap

Top half outer bag

Bottom half outer bag

Assembling the Top and Bottom Pieces

With right sides together, sew the top and bottom fabric pieces together. (**Note:** *The closure strap is attached to the front of the lunch bag, and the handle is attached to the back.*)

Assembling the Drink Pouch

1. Fuse lightweight interfacing to the wrong side of the drink pouch casing strip.

2. With wrong sides together, fold the strip in half widthwise and press. Open the casing strip.

3. Mark the spots for the grommets or buttonholes for the drawstring as follows: On the wrong side of the casing strip, measure ½″ from the folded line and ½″ on either side of the center point. Follow the manufacturer's instructions to insert a small grommet in each hole, or make 2 small machine buttonholes.

4. Baste cording to each short end of the casing and feed through the grommet or buttonhole.

5. With right sides together, fold the casing in half lengthwise and stitch the short ends. Turn right side out and press. The bottom of the casing strip will remain unstitched.

6. With right sides together, pin the open end of the folded casing to the drink pouch, leaving a ½" margin on each side of the pouch. (**Note**: *The grommet side of the casing should face the right side of the pouch.*)

7. Stitch and press the casing.

8. On the drink pouch lining fabric, make a ½" fold along one of the 11" sides, wrong sides together. (This is now the top of the lining.)

9. With right sides together and the top facing up, pin lining to the drink pouch and sew around 3 sides, leaving the top open. Take care not to catch the cording or casing in the seams. Turn right side out and press.

10. Topstitch along the edge of the casing, catching the hemmed lining in the stitching. To create a pleat in the bottom of the drink pouch, on either side of the center point, make a 1" fold by bringing the right sides together.

11. Bring the folded pleats to the center point and press well with steam.

Attaching the Drink Pouch to the Back of the Lunch Bag

1. On the back of the lunch bag, measure up 3" from the bottom and over 3" from the sides.

2. Pin the pleated drink pouch to the back of the bag. Make sure the casing is at the top.

3. Stitch around both sides and the bottom of the drink pouch. Stitch again over the first stitching to provide the pouch with additional strength.

Assembling the Lunch Bag

1. With right sides together, pin the front and the back of the bag along the sides and the bottom. Check to be sure that the sides line up at the seam between the top and bottom fabric pieces and that all straps and cording are tucked out of the way so that they will not get caught in your stitching.

2. Sew both sides of the bag and then sew the bottom of the bag.

3. Bring the bottom corner cuts together, matching the bottom seam and the side seam. Stitch across the corner. Repeat for the other corner. Refer to Corner Construction Techniques on page 118.

4. Turn the bag right side out and press out the bottom seams.

Attaching the Flap

1. With right sides together, center the flap across the top back. (The top back is the side where the handle is attached.)

2. Using a seam allowance just less than ½", stitch across the flap. (This is a basting stitch and will be reinforced once the lining is completed.)

3. Fold the flap over to the front and apply a heavy burst of steam to the seam.

Making the Inside Pocket and Lining

1. Pin the fabrics for the inner pocket right sides together. Using a ¼" seam allowance, stitch down both sides and across the bottom. (Leave the top open for turning.)

2. Turn right side out and press.

3. Fold the pocket binding in half, wrong sides together. Press. Pin the pocket binding strip to the top of the pocket. Fold the raw edges around the upper corners of the pocket.

4. Stitch using a ¼" seam allowance.

5. Press the binding to the wrong side of the pocket and secure with machine or hand stitching.

6. To attach the pocket to the lining fabric, measure up 2½" from the bottom and over 3" from each side. Be certain that the binding is at the top of the pocket. Adjust as necessary to center the pocket.

7. Stitch the pocket to the lining by topstitching along one side, across the bottom, and up the other side.

8. Assemble the lining following the same steps as in "Assembling the Lunch Bag."

Lining the Lunch Bag

1. With right sides together, tuck the lunch bag into the lining. Match up the side seams. Make sure the lining pocket is against the back of the lunch bag.

2. Double-check to make sure the front flap is tucked into the back of the bag and that all cords, straps, and handles are tucked out of the way of your stitching line.

3. Pin the lining in place along the top edges, leaving about a 3" opening for turning in the front of the bag.

4. Stitch around the top of the bag, leaving an opening for turning.

5. Pull the bag and lining right side out through the opening; press.

6. Tuck the lining into the bag. Take care to fold the opening raw edges inside the bag. Press with heavy steam.

7. Topstitch around the top edge of the lunch bag, stitching closed the opening.

FINISHING

1. Fold the flap over to the front. Press with steam, if necessary.

2. Insert the drink pouch drawstring cords through the cord lock following the manufacturer's directions.

3. Pull the closure strap up around the handle.

My lifelong love of sewing has become a fabric-overflowing-the-closet-size hobby. I try to come up with fun, creative ways to use my fabrics and share my ideas. This bag pattern came about because my son had several sets of wood blocks and nothing to store them in. So I designed a fabric basket with a drawstring top. I then realized all the fun possibilities. I downsized the bag, and voilà—lunch bag! Now we have fun fabric lunch bags that are washable and unique to each individual.

www.giddy4paisley.etsy.com

www.giddy4paisley.blogspot.com

MADE BY
Elizabeth Hutton

It's a Cinch

Finished size: 6½″ × 7″ × 3″ (excluding drawstring top)

A sturdy cinch top keeps everything secure and multitasks as convenient handles. With two additional loop handles on the side, this bag is easy to grab and go.

MATERIALS AND CUTTING INSTRUCTIONS

⅝ yard quilter's cotton or home decor weight for bag and handles:

- Cut 1 rectangle 18″ × 21″ for bag.
- Cut 2 rectangles 3″ × 7″ for handles.

⅞ yard quilter's cotton or home decor
weight for lining, top fabric, and drawstrings:

- Cut 1 rectangle 18″ × 21″ for lining.
- Cut 2 rectangles 11″ × 9″ for drawstring top.

- Cut 3 strips 2" × 18" for drawstrings.
  Subcut 1 strip in half to make 2 pieces 2" × 9".

18" × 21" rectangle batting or interfacing (optional)

Chalk or fabric pen

Safety pin

CONSTRUCTION

Note: *All seam allowances are ¼" unless otherwise noted. Press all seams as you go.*

Trimming the Corners

Stack the 18" × 21" rectangles from the main fabric, lining, and batting. From each rectangle, cut a 7" square from each corner (these are scraps).

Sewing the Outer Bag

1. Baste or fuse the batting/interfacing to the wrong side of the main fabric.

2. Fold the main fabric right sides together to match the 2 adjacent corner edges along the raw edges. Stitch from the top raw edges to the corner.

3. Repeat Step 2 with the 3 remaining corners.

4. If you are using quilt batting, trim off any excess along the top edge and from the seam allowances.

Sewing the Lining

Note: *Use a ½" seam allowance.*

1. Repeat Steps 1–3 under Sewing the Outer Bag with the lining fabric, but on the last corner, leave a 4" opening in the middle of the seam. Make sure to

backstitch at the beginning and end of this opening. This opening will be used for turning the bag right side out.

2. Iron the last seam open to make a nice and easy hand-stitch seam guide.

Sewing the Handles

1. With right sides together, fold the first handle in half lengthwise; press. Sew along the long raw edge.

2. Turn the handle right side out, press, and topstitch with a ⅛" seam allowance down the length of each side.

3. Repeat Steps 1 and 2 for the second handle.

Sewing the Top

1. With the right side of the drawstring top facing up, fold a 9" × 11" rectangle in half lengthwise; press.

2. With the wrong side facing up, fold each 9" side in ½" and press.

3. Repeat Steps 1 and 2 for the second rectangle.

4. Unfold and pin the 2 rectangles together, right sides together, making sure to match up the center fold line.

5. With chalk, a fabric marker, or pins, mark ½" on each side of the center crease line and then ¾" from that mark. Repeat the markings on the other pinned side of the rectangle. Begin sewing your seam, stopping when you come to the first mark. Leaving a ¾" opening, reposition and start sewing at the next mark and stop when you get to the next mark. Reposition again to begin sewing at the last mark.

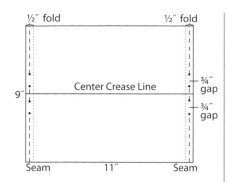

½″ fold   ½″ fold

Center Crease Line

9″

¾″ gap

¾″ gap

Seam   11″   Seam

6. Press the seams open.

7. Topstitch down each side of the seam, using a ⅛″ seam allowance. Repeat for the second seam.

8. Turn the top right side out and fold in half along the center crease line; press.

9. Following the top fold, topstitch with a ½″ seam allowance around the entire top. Next topstitch ¾″ from the previous seam, creating a tunnel for the drawstrings.

Sewing the Drawstrings

1. Join a 2″ × 18″ strip to a 2″ × 9″ strip to form one long drawstring. Place the 18″ strip right side up. Then place the 9″ strip wrong side up perpendicular to the 18″ strip, matching the edges.

2. Attach the 2 strips by sewing from one corner to the opposite at a 45° angle.

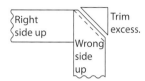

Right side up

Wrong side up

Trim excess.

3. Trim the seam allowance to ¼″. Press the seam open.

4. Fold the strip in half lengthwise, with wrong sides together, and press. Unfold it and then fold each side in to meet the fold line; press. Fold it in half lengthwise and press.

5. Topstitch down the open long side, using a ⅛″ seam allowance.

6. Repeat Steps 1–5 with the second set of strips.

Assembling the Lunch Bag

1. With the main fabric bag right side out, sew the handles into place on the short (3½″) sides of the bag.

2. Make your lunch bag sandwich layers, starting with the outermost fabric:

Main fabric bag wrong side out

Top

Lining right side out

Match up the raw edges and corners, pin in place, and sew through all the layers together with a ½″ seam allowance.

3. Turn right side out and press.

4. Topstitch around the very top of the lunch bag.

5. Insert a drawstring tie. Attach a safety pin to one end of the tie and feed it through the tunnel all the way around the top, ending on the same side as you started. Tie or sew the loose ends together so they don't get pulled back through.

6. Repeat Step 5 with the second string but enter from the opposite opening.

7. Hand stitch the opening in the lining closed, using a hidden slip-stitch or ladder stitch.

I named my handbag company, May.tree.ark, after my grandmother May, whose values of perfection and dedication to making useful things are the soul of my business. My handmade bags are simple yet sophisticated. Each is built with organization in mind—to tote around our modern marvels like cell phones and iPods, all while looking charming.

www.maytreeark.etsy.com

MADE BY
Catherine Janda

The Rita May

Finished size: 9″ × 7″ × 4″

Carry your newspaper, yoga mat, or picnic blanket in style with this cleverly designed bag. Two sturdy shoulder straps extend below the bag to hold rolled items. Choose a fun focus fabric for the large front pocket.

MATERIALS AND CUTTING INSTRUCTIONS

½ yard light brown fabric for exterior:

- Cut 2 squares 12″ × 12″ for bag exterior.

½ yard dark brown fabric for interior lining:

- Cut 2 squares 12″ × 12″ for bag interior lining.

¼ yard newsprint fabric for pocket:

- Cut 2 rectangles 6″ × 8″ for pocket.

3¾ yards black belting strap:

- Cut 2 pieces 65″ each

¾ yard fusible interfacing:

- Cut 2 squares 12″ × 12″ for bag exterior.
- Cut 2 rectangles 6″ × 8″ for pocket.

Water-soluble fabric marker

CONSTRUCTION

Note: All seam allowances are ¼".

Making the Body

1. Iron fusible interfacing to the wrong sides of the light brown fabric and the newsprint fabric.

2. Mark the 4 corners of each light brown fabric square for pocket and strap positioning. On the right side of the fabric, mark 2 dots, each 3" from the top edge and 2" from each side edge. Mark 2 more dots 4" from the bottom edge and 2" from each side edge. Repeat with the other light brown fabric square.

3. Mark 2" squares in the bottom corners of each light brown fabric. These small squares will be cut out later to create the bag's gusset.

4. Repeat Step 3 on the dark brown fabric.

Assembling the Bag

Pocket

1. Place the newsprint fabric pieces right sides together. Pin along the top and bottom, but not the sides.

2. Sew the top and bottom. Turn the pocket right side out at either side and press, leaving the sides rough.

3. Place the pocket on the light brown fabric at the 4 marked dots; pin in place.

4. Stitch the pocket to the light brown fabric at the sides and bottom.

Straps

1. Sew all 4 ends of the black belting strap to eliminate any unraveling.

2. Measure and mark 15" up from all 4 ends of the strips.

3. Pin the strap, from the bottom edge, along the pocket's raw side edges up to the 15" strap mark. Repeat on the other side of the light brown fabric.

4. Using black thread, stitch the belting strap to the bag, starting at the top mark and moving down to the bottom mark and then back up the other side. Backstitch at the top.

5. Pin the straps (now the handle and ties) to the body of the bag to keep them out of the way.

Assembling the Body

1. Place the right sides of the light brown fabric squares together. Pin and sew at the sides and bottom.

2. Cut out the 2" × 2" marked corners.

3. Pinch the corners right sides together. Pin and sew to create the 4" gusset. Refer to Corner Construction Techniques on page 118.

Making the Interior Lining

1. Repeat Steps 1–3 for "Making the Body," using the lining fabric. However, leave one corner unstitched for later turning.

FINISHING

1. Turn the light brown fabric right side out; leave the dark brown fabric inside out. Place them right sides together.

2. Pin the 2 pieces together around the top. Sew.

3. Turn the bag by pulling the light brown fabric through the gusset corner opening of the lining.

4. Pinch, pin, and sew closed the dark brown fabric's corner.

5. Stuff the dark brown interior inside the bag. Iron around the top.

6. *Optional:* Topstitch around the top and along the side.

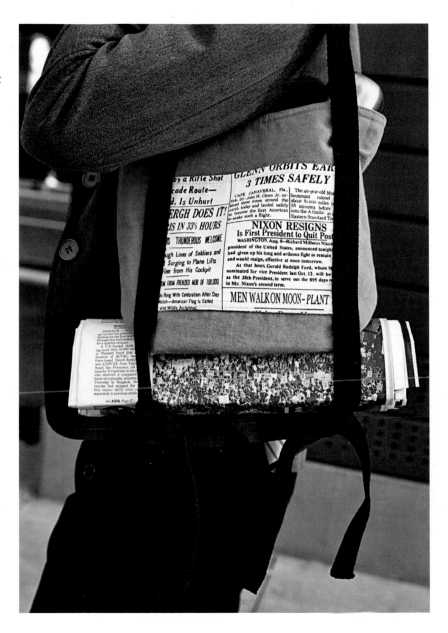

I grew up with a creative mom who taught me very early the ins and outs of a sewing machine and the rewards and satisfaction of creating. When my own daughter was born, she became the inspiration behind my Busy Little Hands business, where I sell blankets, totes, and other handmade items for children. Seeing what interests my daughter, I have designed toys and accessories to make children's lives more fun. With all the toy recalls, it is nice to know how and where things are made. And they are always handmade with love.

www.busylittlehands.net

MADE BY
Janice Kalin

Busy Mama's Sandwich Wrap

Finished size: 15¼″ × 15¼″

Whether wrapping a bagel for work or a sandwich for lunch, a laminated cotton wrap saves on disposable bags and adds a bit of color to the day. The button closure prevents spills and the laminated cotton interior can simply be wiped clean.

MATERIALS AND CUTTING INSTRUCTIONS

1 fat quarter cotton fabric:

- Cut 1 square 16″ × 16″. Cut 4″ off each corner at a 45° angle to make an octagon.

18″ × 18″ square oilcloth:

- Cut 1 square 16″ × 16″. Cut 4″ off each corner at a 45° angle to make an octagon.

2″ × 2″ square fusible interfacing

1″ button

2″-diameter hair elastic

Fabric marker

CONSTRUCTION

Note: *All seam allowances are ⅜″, unless otherwise noted.*

Attaching the Button and Elastic

1. Fold the cotton fabric in half, right sides together, to find the center line. Measure 5½″ from the top along the center line and mark this spot with the fabric marker. This will be the button spot.

2. Use the fabric marker to mark the center line at the bottom edge of the fabric. This will be the elastic spot.

3. Unfold the cotton fabric, wrong side up. Center the 2″ × 2″ fusible interfacing over the button mark. Fuse the interfacing to the wrong side of the fabric.

4. Turn over the fabric to the right side and attach the button on the button mark.

5. Pin the elastic to the center line mark at the bottom of the fabric. The elastic should have a 1″ loop toward the middle of the fabric. Baste the elastic to the edge of the fabric.

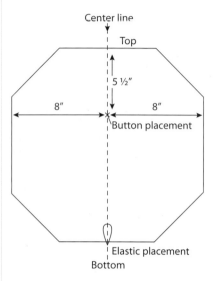

Assembling the Sandwich Wrap

1. Place the cotton fabric and oilcloth right sides together. Use a short stitch to sew around the outside, leaving a 4″ opening.

2. Turn the sandwich wrap right side out through the 4″ opening. Use a chopstick or pencil to carefully push out the sharp corners.

3. Fold in the seam allowance of the 4″ opening and finger-press. Do not use an iron.

4. Use a ¼″ seam allowance to topstitch around the outside of the sandwich wrap.

Folding the Completed Sandwich Wrap

1. With the oilcloth side up, place the sandwich in the middle of the wrap. Fold in each side over the sandwich.

2. Fold the top of the wrap over the sandwich.

3. Fold the bottom of the wrap up over the sandwich and fasten the elastic over the button.

Cleaning and Care

1. Wipe the oilcloth after each use with soap and water or vinegar.

2. Spot clean the fabric with soap and water.

3. Store with the oilcloth facing out.

4. Do not put in the dryer.

I am a stay-at-home mom to one very active little boy living in Vancouver, Washington. Having grown up around crafting and sewing of all kinds, I later gained a love of quilting and fabric hoarding. I enjoy many forms of creating: fabric, yarn, paper, and digital photography, to name just a few. I enjoy creating tutorials that are easy to follow and that will get people crafting.

www.thesometimescrafter.com

Denim Lunch Bag

MADE BY
Christina Lane

Finished size: 11″ × 11″ × 5″

This bag is full of charming details that offer a home for everything. From the inside polka dot pocket to the double-ribbon tie closure to the exterior pocket with accent trim, it's all in the thoughtful details with this bag.

MATERIALS AND CUTTING INSTRUCTIONS

½ yard 54″-wide denim fabric for bag exterior:

Cut 1 strip 11½″ × 54½″ and crosscut as follows:

- Cut 2 squares 11½″ × 11½″ for front and back.
- Cut 2 strips 11½″ × 5″ for sides.
- Cut 1 strip 11½″ × 8½″ for exterior pocket.
- Cut 2 strips 11½″ × 2½″ for handles.
- Cut 1 strip 12″ × 5½″ for bottom.

½ yard 44″-wide medium red dot fabric for lining:

- Cut 1 strip 11½″ × 44″ and crosscut as follows:
    Cut 2 squares 11½″ × 11½″ for front and back.

- Cut 2 strips 11½" × 5" for sides.
- Cut 2 strips 11½" × 2½" for handles.
- Cut 1 strip 12" × 5½" for bottom.

11½" × 9½" strip small red dot fabric for exterior pocket lining

8" × 10" strip small green dot fabric for interior pocket

2 lengths of 24" ribbon in red and green for ties:

- Cut 2 lengths 12" each from each color for ties.

1¼ yard 20"-wide fusible interfacing:

- Cut 2 squares 11½" × 11½" for front and back.
- Cut 2 strips 11½" × 5" for sides.
- Cut 1 strip 12" × 5½" for bottom.
- Cut 1 strip 11½" × 8½" for exterior pocket.
- Cut 2 strips 2½" × 11½" for handles.
- Cut 1 strip 8" × 5" for interior pocket.

CONSTRUCTION

Note: *All seam allowances are ¼".*

Assembling the Handles

1. Iron the fusible interfacing to the wrong side of the denim handle pieces.

2. Place the denim and medium red dot handle fabrics together, right sides together. Sew along the length of each side of the strips, leaving the ends unsewn.

3. Turn each handle right side out and press.

4. Topstitch along the long sides of the handles.

Assembling the Exterior

1. Iron the fusible interfacing to the exterior front, back, sides, and bottom pieces, as well as to the lining of the exterior pocket.

2. With right sides together, sew the exterior pocket lining to the denim pocket along the long edges. Press the seam allowances toward the lining. Match up the bottom edges of the 2 fabrics, wrong sides together, and press along the fold. This will leave a little of the lining peaking out over the denim.

3. Baste stitch the exterior pocket to the back denim panel along the sides.

4. Cut a ¼" × ¼" square from each of the 4 corners of the bottom denim piece. Pin the front, back, and side pieces to the bottom piece and sew into place. Press the seam allowances toward the bottom piece.

5. Match an edge of a side panel to the adjacent edge of the front panel, right sides together. Pin in place, making sure the top and bottom corners of the bag pieces match. The bottom of your bag will be tucked up and under a bit when matching the sides. Sew along the length, backstitching at the beginning and end. Repeat this step with the other 3 corners until the bag is formed.

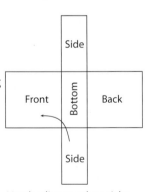

Match adjacent edges, right sides of fabric together.

6. Turn right side out and press the bag on all sides and then along the bottom seams.

Assembling the Lining

1. Iron the interfacing to the interior pocket fabric. The interfacing will cover only half of the pocket fabric. Fold the pocket in half, right sides of fabric together, and stitch along both sides and the bottom, leaving a small opening at the bottom center. Clip the corners. Turn it right side out and press, making sure to press the edges at the opening inward. Edgestitch 2 parallel lines along the folded edge. Starting at the left edge of the pocket, fold and finger-press at 1½″ and 3″.

2. Sew the pocket to one of the lining front/back pieces, topstitching along one side, then the bottom, and finishing on the opposite side. Backstitch at the beginning and end. Create 2 small pockets for utensils and one bigger pocket for a napkin by topstitching at the folds created in Step 1, making sure to backstitch at the beginning and end.

3. Repeat Steps 4 and 5 from "Assembling the Exterior" with lining fabric, leaving a 6″ opening in the middle of a side seam for turning the bag.

FINISHING

1. Attach ribbon ties and handles to the front of the bag, matching raw edges and keeping the right sides of the fabric/ribbons together. Backstitch over the handle and the ribbons a few times to make sure they are securely attached. Repeat to attach ribbon ties and handle to back of the bag.

Note: *To find the positions for the ribbon ties, fold the front piece in half and finger-press. Repeat with the back piece. For handle placement, fold each side of the front and the back into the middle and finger-press the folds. Center the handle ends on the side creases.*

2. Place the exterior of the bag inside the lining, with right sides together and with the interior pocket toward the back of the denim bag. Matching the side seams and top raw edges, pin in place and sew around the top.

3. Turn right side out and use a ladder stitch to sew the opening in the lining closed.

4. Push the lining into the bag and press around the top edge. Topstitch along the top edge, starting and stopping at a seam to disguise your backstitching at the end.

I have enjoyed a lifelong love of creating, from doll dresses and granny square afghans to self-designed knitwear, and finally to sewing fabric accessories. My online store, Blissful, offers fun yet functional wallets and handbags to counteract the preponderance of black apparel. Designs are handcrafted with love and attention to color, detail, and durability. Along with satisfying my creative drive, Blissful gives me a viable reason to continually add to my overflowing stash of Japanese, retro, and floral prints.

www.blissful.etsy.com

www.blissfulbyquenna.blogspot.com

www.flickr.com/photos/blissful

MADE BY
Quenna Lee

Zipper-Top Lunch Bag

Finished size: 8″ × 11″ × 3″

Flawless construction, clean lines, and an easy-to-install zipper closure help make this unfussy lunchbag a success. A canvas bottom for durability, a cotton top for flair, and an insulated lining for practicality make this bag a reliable choice for everyday use.

MATERIALS AND CUTTING INSTRUCTIONS

Note: *Use prewashed cotton fabric if the bag is to be machine washable.*

⅓ yard fabric for outer bag and zipper tab:

- Cut 2 pieces 12″ × 8″ for outer bag.
- Cut 1 piece 3″ × 2″ for zipper tab.

1 fat quarter or ¼ yard denim for bag bottom:

- Cut 2 pieces 12″ × 6″.

½ yard fabric for lining:

- Cut 2 pieces 12″ × 13″.

½ yard ultra-firm interfacing (*substitutions: fleece interfacing, non-wool felt*):

- Cut 2 pieces 11½″ × 13″.

½ yard Insul~Brite (*substitution: same interfacing as above*):

- Cut 2 pieces 11½″ × 13″.

13″–14″ zipper

24″ length of webbing 1″ wide

CONSTRUCTION

Note: *All seam allowances are ⅜″.*

Assembling the Outer Panel

1. With right sides together, sew a 12″ × 8″ piece of outer fabric to a 12″ × 6″ denim bottom piece along the 12″ sides. Repeat with the remaining pieces. Press the seams toward the outer fabric.

2. Pin ultra-firm interfacing to the wrong side of an outer panel. Topstitch near or on the previous seam, going through both layers. Repeat with the other outer panel.

Installing the Zipper

Note: *The right side of the zipper always faces the right sides of the outer panels.*

1. Pin Insul~Brite to the wrong side of the lining fabric.

2. Pin the unzipped zipper to the top of the outer panel, right sides together. The top end of the zipper should line up with the left side of the fabric. Place the lining fabric facedown, sandwiching the zipper in between with the side and top edges aligned. The bottom end of the zipper should extend beyond the fabrics. The order of the fabrics, beginning from the top, is Insul~Brite, lining, wrong side of zipper, outer panel, interfacing.

3. Before sewing, pull the top 1½″ of the zipper about 45° from the fabrics so that it angles upward (to create a tapered end for the zipper). Using a zipper foot, begin sewing 1½″ from the left side seam and stop sewing 1½″ from the right side seam (to create openings for the webbing). The right sides of the outer fabric and lining should face each other.

4. Repeat with the other side of the zipper but with the fabrics in the following order, beginning from the top: interfacing, outer panel, right side of zipper, lining, Insul~Brite. The right sides of the outer fabric and lining should face each other.

Assembling the Bag

1. Flip the pieces so the lining fabrics face each other and the outer panels face each other (right sides together). Make sure the zipper is untwisted and ¾ open. Pin the fabrics together (with the zipper end tucked inside the bag). Trim to even up the edges as needed.

2. Cut 1 square 1½″ × 1½″ from each bottom corner (4 total) to form a flat bottom.

3. At the lining bottom, start sewing 1½″ from the right bottom corner and go all the way around, leaving the corners unsewn until you have reached 1½″ from the opposite corner. This creates the opening for turning the bag right side out. Backstitch whenever the fabric ends and begins (that is, at the cut corners and the corners of the lining and the outer panel). Press the seams open.

4. At the cut corners, pull open until the bottom and side seams meet in the middle. Pin the opening and sew it closed. The stitch line should be perpendicular to the side and bottom seams. Repeat with the remaining 3 corners. Refer to Corner Construction Techniques on pages 118–119.

5. Turn the bag right side out. At the opening, press the fabric ⅜″ inward and sew it closed. Push the lining into the bag and press out at each corner.

6. Press the fabric around the zipper until it is smooth and pulled away from the zipper teeth. At the top openings, press the fabric ½″ inward. Insert webbing into the openings, tucking 1½″ of each end inside. Make sure the zipper end is held away from the webbing (the zipper should lean toward the bag). Pin and stitch all around the top, backstitching at the webbing (stitch slowly, because this is a bulky seam).

7. Trim the excess zipper, if needed. The zipper should extend beyond the side seam. Press the tab fabric ⅜″ all around and fold it in half, wrong sides together. Place the zipper end inside and sew around, fully enclosing it.

Note: *To help keep the lining in place during machine washing, stitch in the ditch 3″–4″ down each side seam, starting from the top.*

After graduating from Michigan State University with a degree in package design, I set to work thinking outside the box. Creating custom boat canvas and interiors was my main focus before I began designing bags and clothing. My current company, Boneshaker Bags, was developed to meet the need for a more aesthetically and environmentally appealing bicycle bag. Boneshaker Bags are made from vintage and reclaimed materials whenever possible, with every bag containing at least 25% recycled materials.

www.boneshakerbags.etsy.com

MADE BY
Joan Leppek

Bicycle Lunch Bag

Finished size: 8″ × 8″ × 3″

A bag designed just for your bike! The clever handles are designed to loop around your handlebars for transport and then be repositioned to function as a carrying handle once you have reached your destination.

MATERIALS AND CUTTING INSTRUCTIONS

½ yard heavyweight fabric for main body of bag, straps, and button flap:

- Cut 1 piece 28″ × 12″ for main body of bag.
- Cut 2 strips 9″ × 3″ for handlebar straps.
- Cut 1 piece 4″ × 3″ for front button flap.

⅓ yard sturdy floral fabric for accent:

- Cut 1 piece 28″ × 6″.

½ yard lighter weight fabric for lining:

- Cut 1 piece 26″ × 12″.

½ yard felt for interfacing:

- Cut 1 piece 28″ × 12″.

⅛ yard fusible interfacing for straps and flap:

- Cut 2 strips 8″ × 2″ for handlebar straps.
- Cut 1 strip 3″ × 2″ for front button flap.

2 buttons (¾″ diameter) with shanks for attaching straps to handlebars

1 button (1¼″ diameter) for front of bag

Chalk for marking seams

CONSTRUCTION

Note: *All seam allowances are ½″.*

Making the Front Button Flap

1. Iron fusible interfacing to the wrong side of the button flap fabric, leaving a ½″ seam allowance exposed on each side.

2. Fold the fabric, right sides together, and sew along the length and one end.

3. Turn, press, and topstitch along the edges, leaving one end unsewn. The finished flap size should be 3½″ × 1″.

4. Make a 1½″-long buttonhole, beginning ¾″ from the finished end of the flap. Cut an opening in the buttonhole.

Making the Handlebar Straps

1. Iron the fusible interfacing to the wrong side of the handlebar strap fabric, leaving a ½″ seam allowance exposed on each side.

2. Fold the fabric, right sides together, and sew along the length and one end.

3. Turn, tuck the unfinished end into the strap, press, and topstitch along the edges. The finished handlebar strap size should be 8″ × 1″.

4. Make 2 buttonholes, each 1″ long, beginning ¾″ from each end of the strap. Use a seam ripper to cut an opening in the buttonholes.

5. Repeat Steps 1–4 with the other handlebar strap.

Making the Lining

1. Fold the lining fabric in half, right sides together.

2. Sew the side seams, leaving a 6″ unsewn section in the middle of one side.

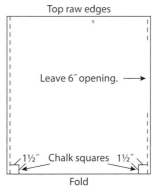

Lining seams

3. Use chalk to draw 1½″ × 1½″ squares inside the seam allowance on the 2 lower corners of the lining. Flip the lining and mark the lower corners on the other side.

4. Fold the side seam toward the bottom crease to turn the chalk "square" into a "triangle."

5. Sew the long side of the triangle.

6. Repeat Steps 4 and 5 on the other corner. Refer to Corner Construction Techniques on pages 118–119.

7. Turn the lining right side out.

Assembling the Main Bag

1. Place the main fabric right side up on top of the felt.

2. Turn under and press ½″ seams on the long sides of the floral accent fabric.

3. Center and pin the wrong side of the accent fabric to the right side of the main fabric and felt. Topstitch the accent fabric to the main fabric and felt.

4. Sew ¾″ buttons 5″ apart and 5″ from the top of the fabric, along the sewn edge of the accent fabric.

5. Center and sew the button flap to the top edge of the fabric, aligning the unfinished button flap edge with the raw edge on top of the fabric. The finished end of the button flap hangs down from the edge with the ¾″ buttons.

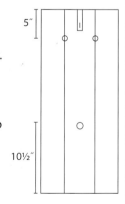

6. Sew a decorative 1¼″ button in the center of the accent fabric strip 10½″ from the bottom edge of the fabric.

7. Fold the main fabric in half, right sides together. Sew the side seams.

8. Draw 1½″ × 1½″ squares inside the seam allowance on the lower corners of the bag. Flip and repeat.

9. Pinch the side seam toward the bottom crease to turn the chalk "square" into a "triangle." Sew the long side of the triangle. Repeat for the other corner.

10. Place the lining into the main bag, right sides together. Sew along the top edge.

11. Reach into the bag and pull the main bag through the opening in the side seam of the lining fabric. Both fabrics are now right side out.

12. Sew the side seam in the lining fabric.

13. Tuck the lining fabric into the main bag.

14. Sew along the inside of the top edge of the bag, rolling the top edge of the main fabric ¼″ into the inside of the bag.

15. Button the handlebar straps to the bag.

I am a self-taught sewer specializing in custom sewing. My primary interest lies in uniting an amazing fabric with a functional item, such as a clothespin apron or grocery bags. I sell to people who are living a lifestyle that believes in buying from small local merchants who are doing what they love—like I am!

www.monsieurcardinale.wordpress.com

MADE BY
Stephanie Lopez

Lunch Bag and Placemat

Finished lunch bag size: 7″ × 10″ × 5″

Finished placemat size: 14½″ × 10½″

Linen, gingham, and cotton combine to make an elegant statement all on their own. But when combined the bag with a placemat, you will have everything necessary for a lunch on the go. This collection set is a breeze to make and invites creative touches, including allowing much-loved fabrics to be showcased.

MATERIALS AND CUTTING INSTRUCTIONS

½ yard natural color linen or linen blend:

- Cut 2 pieces 13″ × 5½″ for outer bag bottom.
- Cut 2 pieces 19″ × 6″ for handles.
- Cut 1 piece 2″ × 2½″ for placemat utensil holder.

½ yard cotton print fabric for outside of bag and one side of placemat:

- Cut 2 pieces 13″ × 9″ for outer bag top.

- Cut 1 piece 11″ × 15″ for placemat.

½ yard coordinating cotton fabric for bag lining, bottle ties, and placemat:

- Cut 2 pieces 13″ × 14″ for lining.
- Cut 2 pieces 12″ × 2″ for bottle ties.
- Cut 1 piece 11″ × 15″ for placemat.

½ yard medium or lightweight fusible interfacing *(optional)*

Disappearing-ink marker

CONSTRUCTION

Note: *All seam allowances are ¼″.*

1. To assemble the outer bag, pin together and sew each outer bag bottom to each outer print piece along the 13″ sides, right sides together. Iron the seam allowances toward the bag bottom side on each of the 2 squares you now have. Topstitch along the edge of the bag bottom where it meets the outer bag top on each square, making sure the sewing machine catches the seam allowances underneath to add reinforcement. Press again. (*Optional step*: If a stiffer bag is desired, iron interfacing according to the manufacturer's directions to the wrong side of the squares. Trim off extra interfacing around the squares.) Sew the squares right sides together along the sides and bottom.

2. To square off the bottom, stand the bag (still wrong side out) and measure 2½″ from the pointy part of the bottom corners of the bag along the side seams. At the 2½″ mark, turn your ruler horizontally and draw a line with a marker. Sew along the marked line and trim off

the corners. Turn the outer bag right side out. Refer to Corner Construction Techniques on pages 118–119.

3. To make the bottle ties, fold each strip lengthwise, wrong sides together. Press. Open each strip, wrong side up. Fold each strip again lengthwise, but this time only halfway on each side, matching the raw edges together in the middle. Press. Fold again lengthwise. Press. You now have 2 double-folded strips. Unfold each strip and press ½″, wrong sides together, on one end of each strip. Double fold the strips again and press. This will create a finished edge on one end of each tie. Sew ⅛″ from the edge of each tie.

4. Pin the lining fabric squares right sides together. As you do this, pin the bottle ties together 6″ down one side, sandwiched between the lining pieces. Sew along the sides and the bottom. Stand the bag lining (still wrong side out) and measure 2½″ from the pointy part of the bottom corners of the bag along the side seams. At the 2½″ mark, turn your ruler horizontally and draw a line with a marker. Sew on the marked line and trim off the corners. Refer to Corner Construction Techniques on pages 118–119.

5. Fold each handle strip lengthwise, wrong sides together. Press. Open each strip, wrong side up. Fold each strip again lengthwise, but this time only halfway on each side, matching the raw edges together in the middle. Then fold the raw edges on the ends of each strip in by ¼″, wrong sides together. Press. Fold again lengthwise. Press. Now you have 2 double-folded strips with all the raw edges folded inside. Sew ⅛″ along the edges of each handle.

6. To assemble the bag, place the lining in the bag, wrong sides together. Finish the top of the bag by folding in the top of the lining by ½″ and folding in the top edge of the outer bag by ½″ so the right sides of the fabric meet. Pin along the top. Sew ⅛″ from the edge. Pin the handles to the bag 3″ from the sides and 2″ from the top edge. Adjust if necessary (if you want to carry the bag on your shoulder, for instance). Sew ⅛″ from the edges of each handle where it meets the bag.

7. Make a utensil holder for the placemat in the same way you made the handles and bottle ties. Sew the holder to the right side of one of the placemat squares, positioned where you would like to have your utensils sit. Sew down each short side of the strip so the utensil can be placed between the 2 stitched ends of the strip. Pin the placemat squares right sides together and sew around the square, leaving a 3″ gap in the middle of one of the sides. Turn the placemat right side out. Press. Hand sew the gap closed. Topstitch around the placemat ½″ from the edges. Press.

I love to sew, create, inspire, share, and, most of all, teach the craft of sewing. Sewing with juice pouches began with a single small purse, and ideas continue to grow into new creations. This lunch bag was created one year during back-to-school time. The side water bottle holder was created to help prevent spills. The sandwich wrap is a new idea to help diminish the use of disposable plastic baggies. I wish all the readers of this book creative sewing!

www.CreativeSews.com

CreativeSewSue (Twitter)

Creative Sewing (Facebook)

MADE BY
Susan Lowe Heaney

Juice Pouch Lunch Bag and Sandwich Wrap

Finished lunch bag size: 9″ × 10½″ × 4″

Finished sandwich wrap size: 11″ × 14″

Recycle and reuse those durable drink pouches to create this stunning duo. The bag has more than just repurposing in mind, with a convenient exterior pocket for a drink bottle and a matching hook-and-loop fastened sandwich wrap to save on all those plastic bags. The interior is easy to clean and is a shining example of eco-friendliness.

MATERIALS

30 juice pouches

Bleach

Goo Gone cleaner

Sewing gauge ruler

Electrical tape

Nonwriting pen or dull pin

2″ length of sew-on hook-and-loop tape

2 sticky-back hook-and-loop coins

Flexible fabric glue

22″ length of nylon webbing 1″ wide

Water bottle

PREPARATION

1. Uniformly trim each juice pouch to 5″ tall. Excess measurement should be trimmed from the top of the pouch. It is important that all the juice pouches are even and the same size! Open the pouches and rinse with hot water. Soak in a solution of hot water and bleach. Thoroughly rinse each pouch and stand it upside down to dry. Use Goo Gone cleaner to remove any glue spots.

2. Set your sewing machine to a narrow-length zigzag stitch, unless otherwise noted. All seam allowances will be measured using the sewing gauge ruler and marked with the tip of a blunt object, such as a nonwriting pen or a dull pin. Accuracy of these markings is important

for alignment and fit. Always backstitch at the beginning and end of sewing. Stitching should always be done on the right (printed) side of the pouches. Tape should be removed as you sew.

CONSTRUCTING THE SANDWICH WRAP

1. Place 9 cleaned juice pouches right side down in 3 rows of 3. Mark a ¼″ seam allowance on the right edge of the first 2 pouches in each row. Overlap the left edge of the neighboring pouches with the seam allowance markings.

2. Tape the pouches in place and stitch the overlap, right side up. Continue this assembly for the 3 rows of 3.

3. Along the bottom edge of the first row, mark a ¼″ seam allowance on the wrong side. Align the top edge of the second row with this mark. Tape it in place on the right side and stitch. Repeat for the bottom row.

4. You should now have a sheet of 9 pouches sewn in 3 rows of 3. Stitch across the very top edge to close the openings.

Placing the hook-and-loop tape

1. Trim the loop side of a 2″ piece of hook-and-loop tape to 1⅛″. Keep the hook side at 2″.

2. With the right side up, turn the sheet so the writing is facing you upside down. On the bottom edge, center the loop side of the tape ¾″ in from the edge, perpendicular to the bottom edge. Set your machine to a straight stitch and sew in place along all 4 sides of the tape.

3. On the wrong side of the top of the sheet, center the hook side of the tape ½" in from the edge so that 1½" extends beyond the edge. Only ½" of tape will be sewn onto the pouch. Double-check that you have aligned the hook-and-loop tape by folding the sheet in half to ensure that the proper sides of the tape meet. Sew the tape in place along 4 sides.

Scoring the Creases

1. On the wrong side, mark 2⅛" in along each long side of the sheet. Fold and crease along these lines.

2. Fold under each corner at an angle approximately 1" from the edge to form 4 triangles. These corners will be tucked under each time the wrap is folded closed.

3. Mark 4" from the bottom edge. Fold and crease in place.

4. Fold the top edge down so the hook-and-look tape aligns. Finger-press. This can be adjusted according to the sandwich size.

CONSTRUCTING THE LUNCH BAG WITH WATER BOTTLE HOLDER

Note: *Use 21 cleaned juice pouches for construction.*

Front, Back, and Flap (12 pouches)

1. Place 4 pouches, wrong side up, to form 2 rows of 2.

2. On the right edge of the upper-left pouch, mark a ¼" seam allowance. Overlap the neighboring pouch so it is even with the seam allowance marking. Tape it in place and stitch the overlap, right side up. Repeat for the remaining 2 pouches.

3. On the wrong side of the bottom edge of the top row of pouches, mark a ¼" seam allowance. Align the top edge of the other set of pouches with the marked seam allowance. Tape in place and stitch the over-lapped area, right side up. Repeat this step to create 2 additional sets. When this step is complete, you should have 3 separate sheets of 4 pouches.

4. For the lunch bag front, sew across the very top of a sheet to close the opening.

5. For the flap, trim 1½″ from the top edge of the sheet. Along the bottom edge, stitch a rounded curve. Trim the excess pouch away from the curve.

6. Mark a ½″ seam allowance along the top edge of the flap. Align the top edge of the remaining sheet, tape, and stitch. This is the back and front flap.

Sides (4 pouches)

1. Mark a ¼″ seam allowance on the bottom of 1 pouch. Align the top edge of a second pouch with this seam allowance marking. The pouches will be stacked one on top of the other. Tape and stitch.

2. Stitch across the very top pouch opening.

3. Repeat Steps 1 and 2 for side 2.

4. Set your machine to a straight stitch. Match the thread color to the web handle.

5. Find the midpoint of the top edge of the pouch side. Make a mark 1″ from the top edge midpoint and another mark 2″ below the top edge midpoint.

6. Align the webbing at the 2″ mark. Use tape to hold the webbing in place. Sew up to the 1″ mark, completing a 1″ square. Sew an × inside the 1″ square.

7. Repeat Steps 4–6 for the other side with the opposite end of the webbing. Ensure that the web handle is not twisted. Two completed sides are now connected to the web handle.

Bottom (2 pouches)

1. Reset your machine to a zigzag setting. Place the completed lunch bag front on a flat surface. To create the bag bottom, place 2 pouches right sides up. Overlap *lengthwise* to a width even with the completed front. Tape and sew. Trim the excess of the overlap from the wrong side.

2. Align an edge of the sewn bottom with the lunch bag front, wrong sides together. Sew.

3. Attach the remaining bottom edge to the lunch bag back, wrong sides together, in the same manner. The front and back attached to the bottom are now complete. Finger-press along the seams.

Bottle Holder Bottom and Sides Attachment (1 pouch)

1. Lay the completed portion of the bag flat, wrong side up, with the front closest to you.

2. Slide a new pouch all the way under the right edge of the bottom of the bag, until the right edge of the bag bottom and the right edge of the new pouch align. The added pouch should be right side up with the straw holder end to the right

3. Take the completed right side with a web handle. Align the bottom edge to the *bag bottom*, wrong sides together. Sew these 3 layers together. (The bottom layer is 1 juice pouch, wrong side down. The middle layer is the bottom of the bag. The top layer is the side of the bag, right side up.) Sew all 3 layers together, keeping them evenly aligned. Do not sew through the existing seams on the bag. Begin and end sewing just inside these areas.

4. Make sure that the handle is not twisted and then sew the opposite side to the bag bottom. There will only be 2 layers to sew on this side.

5. Align the long front edge of a side with the bag front. Stitch.

6. Align the 3 remaining sides and stitch.

Side Bottle Holder (2 pouches)

1. Set your machine to the straight stitch setting. Take the remaining 2 pouches and place them right sides together. Sew a ½" seam along the long edge. Trim the seam. Finger-press the seam open.

2. Return your machine to the zigzag setting. Stitch across the very top edge of these 2 pouches.

Attaching the Bottle Holder to the Bag

1. Align the bottle-holder pouches with the bottom of the right side of the bag. Sew this to the bag at the front and back edges.

2. Finger-press the floor pouch out to the side. The wrong side should be facing up.

3. Place a bottle in the holder and form-press to shape. Trace the semicircular shape on the bottom pouch. Add ⅜" extra for a seam allowance. It is necessary to scrunch the bottom edges to fit as evenly together as possible. This is not an exact fit.

4. Sew the bottom edges together, wrong sides together. It may be necessary to trim extra areas from the pouch after sewing.

FINISHING

1. Form-shape all areas of the lunch bag.

2. Attach 2 sticky-back hook-and-loop coins to the front and the flap. Reinforce with flexible fabric glue.

I taught myself to sew 14 years ago, and it's the best addiction a girl can have. My designs come from a desire to add a bit of comfort and a bit of whimsy to my day. I find inspiration in pretty much everything. A touch, smell, or beautiful fabric is usually enough to get the spark going. I get such a thrill when people who have bought my items take the time to write a note telling me how much they love them. My hope is to continue to design and create until the sun gives up its rays.

www.sandrakay.etsy.com

www.sandrakaycreations.com

www.flickr.com/photos/skepole

MADE BY
Sandra Kay McCormick

Lunch Sack with Apple Appliqué

Finished size: 9″ × 10½″ × 3″

It doesn't get much simpler than this button-close top. When the basic bag is so quick to make, personalization using names, letters, favorite characters, and more is easy. Add fun appliqué designs and embellishments, or even let your child paint some fabric before you sew to create a one-of-a-kind project.

MATERIALS AND CUTTING INSTRUCTIONS

Note: *Apple appliqué pattern on page 123.*

⅓ yard denim fabric for lunch sack:

- Cut 2 of pattern for lunch sack.

½ yard red 100% cotton gingham fabric for lining of lunch sack, apple appliqué, loop for closing back, and button cover:

- Cut 2 of pattern for lining.
- Cut 1 strip 1¾″ × 5″ for loop.
- Cut 1 apple for appliqué.

Scrap of green fabric for leaf appliqué:

- Cut 1 leaf.

Scrap of brown fabric for apple stem appliqué:

- Cut 1 stem.

1 size-36 (⅞″) half-ball covered button

CONSTRUCTION

Note: *All seam allowances are ½″. Prewash all fabric.*

Red Gingham Loop for Lunch Sack Closure

1. Fold the strip of loop fabric in half lengthwise, wrong sides together, and press.

2. Open the strip and place it wrong side up. Fold the left side of the fabric to the center lengthwise and press. Fold the right side of the fabric to the center lengthwise and press. Fold in half lengthwise and press.

3. Stitch closed close to the edge. Trim the strip to 3½″.

Constructing the Lunch Sack

1. Center the loop on the top of the back of the lunch sack.

2. Sew in place close to the edge.

3. Cover the button with a scrap of red gingham fabric. Sew the button to the front of the lunch sack, 7½″ down from the top and centered.

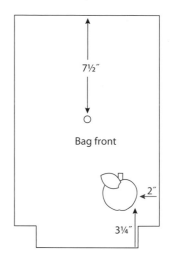

4. Position the apple appliqué on the front of the lunch sack 3¼″ up from the bottom and 2″ in from the right side.

5. Sew the appliqué in place.

6. Place the front and back denim right sides together. Sew the side and bottom seams.

7. Create the bottom of the bag by matching the side seam to the bottom seam.

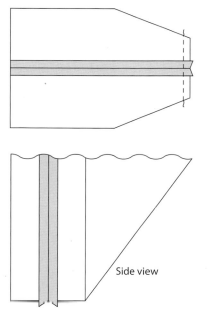

Side view

8. Stitch using a ½″ seam allowance. Press open the seams.

9. Turn the bag right side out.

Constructing the Lining

1. Place the front and back lining pieces right sides together. Sew the side seams.

2. Sew the bottom seam, leaving a 3½″ centered opening for turning.

3. Create the bottom of the lining by joining the side seam to the bottom seam, as you did for the outer bag.

4. Press the seams open.

Assembling the Lunch Sack

1. Keeping the lining wrong side out and the lunch sack right side out, slip the lining over the lunch sack, right sides together. Make sure the loop is tucked inside. Sew around the top.

2. Turn the lunch sack by pulling it through the opening in the lining. Sew closed the lining opening.

3. Push the lining into the lunch sack and press flat. Topstitch around the top of the bag.

4. Fold down the top of the bag 3¼″ and press flat.

5. Pull the button through the loop to close the bag.

It all began when Grandma gave me my first crochet hook in kindergarten. I've always had the undeniable urge to create. As a child, times were tough, but that didn't stop me. From dryer-lint Barbie wear to toilet-paper Christmas ornaments, I always stayed creative, using whatever materials I could find. These days I cannot sit through a movie or long car trip without some project in hand. My focus is on creating items that support a sustainable lifestyle.

Rural western Pennsylvania is my home, where I live a blissful life with my husband of ten years and our two darling little boys.

www.uniquerabbit.etsy.com

MADE BY
Kimberly Paglia

Earth-Friendly Snack Baggies

Finished size: 7″ × 6½″

These hook-and-loop closure snack bags make the perfect companion to any of the larger lunch bags in the book. You'll want to make a bunch for holding everything from crackers to dried fruit. You'll never use plastic again!

MATERIALS

Makes 2 baggies.

14½″ × 14½″ square outer print fabric

14½″ × 14½″ square lining fabric (7–oz. organic cotton canvas recommended)

½ yard sew-on hook-and-loop tape

CONSTRUCTION

Note: *All seam allowances are ¼" unless otherwise noted.*

1. Place the fabric and lining squares right sides together.

2. Cut this square in half vertically so that you have 2 sets of rectangular-shaped baggies.

3. With right sides facing, sew the pieces together along the top and bottom.

4. Turn the bag right side out and iron the seams flat.

5. Sew a piece of hook-and-loop tape (hook side) to the print side, ½" from the edge.

6. Sew another piece of hook-and-loop tape (loop side) to the lining side of the baggie, ⅛" from the edge.

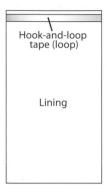

7. Fold the baggie so the print side is facing out. However, the flap of the lining that has the loop tape on it should be folded down over the back so that it aligns with the hook tape on the print side.

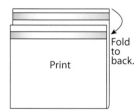

8. I use a serger to finish the side seams. You can also just sew them and then finish the raw edges with a zigzag stitch.

Caring for Wraps and Baggies

Machine wash and dry. Turn the bags inside out and close the hook-and-loop tape before washing to prevent the tape from sticking to other items in the wash.

You can use these bags over and over again before washing—just shake out the crumbs. If you have something particularly messy, you may choose to line the wrap with a piece of waxed paper, foil, or plastic wrap. The liner will keep the mess contained, and the wrap will hold everything nice and secure in your lunch bag. This liner can then be wiped clean and reused many times.

I launched Bugga Bugs—Heart-Felt Fun in the spring of 2008. This pattern shop is dedicated to childhood imagination and creativity. Popular in the pattern world are my simple step-by-step instructions and beautiful photography. My patterns create items that turn out beautifully time and time again, even for the novice.

Always on the lookout for my latest designs, I find inspiration in the everyday and deem that the greatest insight for my creations comes from my children. Hailing from a long line of designers, I tapped into my roots and brought my mother, Veanne, and sister, Angie, onto the team. Our threesome enjoys putting our collective talent to good purpose— inspiring moms everywhere to play with and educate their children.

www.buggabugs.blogspot.com

www.etsy.com/shop/buggabugs

MADE BY
Annika Rau

Sack Lunch

Finished sack size: 6¾" × 8⅜" × 2½"

Finished sandwich size: 4" × 4" × ½"

Finished banana peel size: 6¾" × 1¾"

Finished cookie size: 2½" × 2½" × 1"

A felt lunch set is fun to make just for play. This balanced meal features a banana, a cookie, and a sandwich that contains separate slices of cheese, lunch meat, tomato, and a lettuce leaf. All fit perfectly in the 'paper sack.'

MATERIALS AND CUTTING INSTRUCTIONS

Note: *Patterns are on pages 124–127.*

Felt sheets (available in 9″ × 12″):

4 cream:

- Cut 4 bread slices.
- Cut 2 bananas (1 and 1 reversed).
- Cut 2 banana peels (1 and 1 reversed).

5 tan:

- Cut 2 strips 1¼″ × 16″ for bread crusts. (*If you are using craft felt sheets, the crusts may need to be pieced together to form long strips.*)
- Cut 2 rectangles 7″ × 8½″ for lunch bag front and back.
- Cut 1 rectangle 7″ × 2¾″ for lunch bag bottom.
- Cut 2 rectangles 8½″ × 2¾″ for lunch bag side panels.

1 pink:

- Cut 2 ham slices.

2 yellow:

- Cut 2 cheese slices.
- Cut 2 banana peels (1 and 1 reversed).

1 red:

- Cut 2 tomato slices.
- Cut 4 tomato seeds.

1 green:

- Cut 2 lettuce leaves.

1 dark brown or black:

- Cut 4 cookies.
- Cut 1 banana tip.

1 white:

- Cut 1 cookie filling.

Fiberfill for stuffing

Water-soluble fabric marker for tracing

CONSTRUCTION

Note: *All seam allowances are ¼".*

Sandwich Bread

1. Beginning at a bottom corner, sew a crust piece around the top of a bread piece, stopping at the other bottom corner. Trim off any excess, leaving a ¼" seam allowance.

2. Sew the excess crust to the bottom of the bread piece by matching the corners of the crust pieces to square the corners; then sew in place. Trim any remaining felt.

3. Pin and sew the second bread piece to the top of the crust, leaving an opening for turning. Turn the bread right side out.

4. Lightly stuff the bread with fiberfill. Hand stitch the opening closed.

5. Repeat Steps 1–4 to make a total of 2 slices of bread.

Ham

1. Sew around the edges of 2 ham pieces, leaving an opening for turning.

2. Turn the ham right side out. Hand stitch the opening closed.

3. Give the ham some character by topstitching ¼" around the edges.

Cheese

1. Sew 2 felt cheese pieces around the edges, leaving an opening for turning.

2. Turn the cheese right side out. Hand stitch the opening closed.

3. Give the cheese some character by topstitching ¼" around the edges.

Lettuce

1. Stitch together 2 lettuce leaves around the edges, leaving an opening for turning.

2. Turn the lettuce right side out. Hand stitch the opening closed.

3. Sew lines down the lettuce, as shown on the pattern.

Tomato

1. Stitch 2 tomato slices together around the edges, leaving an opening for turning.

2. Turn the tomato slice right side out. Hand stitch the opening closed.

3. Hand stitch the 4 seed triangles onto the tomato top.

Banana

1. Place a cream felt banana peel on top of a yellow felt banana peel. Sew around the edges, leaving an opening for turning. Repeat for the other side of the banana peel.

2. Turn the banana peels right sides out. Place the peels on top of each other, with the yellow sides in. Sandwich the brown tip between the peels at the bottom.

3. Sew around the peels, leaving the top third open so the peel can be folded back. Trim off any excess brown at the bottom.

4. Stitch 2 cream banana pieces around the edges, leaving an opening for turning. Turn the banana right side out.

5. Firmly stuff the banana with fiberfill and hand stitch the opening closed.

6. Turn the banana peel right side out and place the banana inside.

Chocolate Cookie

1. Stitch 2 cookie pieces together around the edges, leaving an opening for turning. Repeat with the remaining 2 cookie pieces.

2. Turn the cookies right sides out. Hand stitch the openings closed. Topstitch ¼" around each edge.

3. Sew the short ends of the cream center strip together, using a ¼"–¾" seam. Use the smaller seam option to create a more filled-looking cookie and the larger seam for a more thinly filled cookie.

4. Turn the cream right side out and hand sew between the 2 cookies, using clear thread and leaving an opening for stuffing. Stuff the cookie with fiberfill, then sew the opening closed.

5. Double thread your needle with black thread. Following the marks on the cookie pattern, tie a knot on the cookie top, then pull the thread through to the opposite side and tie another. Continue all around the cookie. This will add interest.

Sack

1. Sew 1½″ from the edge of the front and back panels to give them character.

2. Use pinking sheers to cut the top edges of the front, back, and side panels.

3. Sew the side panels to the front and back panels, using a ⅛″ seam.

4. Sew the bottom piece to the bag, using a ⅛″ seam.

5. Turn the bag right side out and sew up the seams ¼″ to hide the seams inside. This also gives the bag stability.

I create at Dayshift, my very own studio and boutique in Carbondale, Illinois. Dayshift proudly features multiple local artists' work. You can also find the hobo cinch, as well as many of my other handmade goodies, on my Etsy site.

www.inblue.etsy.com

Hobo Cinch

MADE BY
Mary Lynn Schroeder

Finished size: 21″ × 16″ (not cinched)

Easy to make, easy to pack, and easy to carry, this larger bag is ideal for small picnics. With a cinch top and a broad single panel on the bottom, this bag is contemporary enough to fit in at a concert or at the beach, yet still smart enough for the office.

MATERIALS AND CUTTING INSTRUCTIONS

½ yard fabric for outside shell of bag (*home decor fabric, twill, canvas, printed cotton, or solid fabric*):

- Cut 2 rectangles 20″ × 14″. Curve a "U" shape by tracing the curve of a plate on the bottom of 2 corners. The finished shape should be 20″ across the top and 14″ tall in the middle.

½ yard lining fabric (*ripstop nylon or cotton*):

- Use the outside pieces as a pattern to create 2 "U" shaped pieces for the lining.

¼ yard fabric for casing around the straps at the top of the bag (*twill, corduroy, cotton, canvas, or any home decor fabric*):

- Cut 2 rectangles 8″ × 18″ for casing.

70″ length of coordinating cotton webbing for straps:

- Cut into 2 pieces 35″ each.

CONSTRUCTION

Note: *All seam allowances are ½".*

Assembling the Casing

1. Iron and hem in the 8" ends of your casing rectangles by ½". This will be the only stitching that will show on the outside of your bag, so go ahead and have fun with it. Use a decorative stitch if you like!

2. Fold and iron the rectangles in half, wrong sides together, so they measure 4" tall and 17" across.

3. Center the raw edges of the rectangles even with the right side of the top of your outside fabric, leaving approximately 1½" on either end of the outside half-circle, and pin in place. Baste a rectangle into place on each half-circle piece along the top raw edges.

Assembling the Outside Fabric

1. Place the half-circles together, right sides facing, and pin.

2. Stitch the half-circles together, from the top end of the half-circle down and around the whole curve of the piece to the other top end of the half circle, leaving the top (straight edge) open. Clip your curves, but leave the outside shell inside out (you will be turning it later).

Assembling the Lining

1. Place the half-circles of lining together, right sides facing, and pin in place.

2. Stitch the half-circles together, leaving a 3" gap at the bottom of the bag for turning. Remember to backstitch at either end of the 3" gap. Leave the top straight edge open, as you did for the outside fabric. Clip your curves and turn this piece right side out.

Putting It Together

1. Place the lining fabric (right sides out) inside the outer shell (still inside out) and casing fabric piece, so that the right sides of the lining face the right sides of the outside fabric.

2. Pin the lining to the outside fabric and stitch all the way around the top edges of the bag.

3. Pull the outside shell through the gap at the bottom of the lining fabric, turning the whole bag right side out.

4. Press the raw edges of the 3″ gap at the bottom of the lining in; stitch up the gap. Then push the lining inside the bag. You are almost finished!

Last (but not least): The Straps

Thread a 35″ piece of cotton webbing through the casing on one side of the top of the bag (make sure the webbing is not twisted). Sew the ends together with a 1½″ overlap. (I like to use a repetitive zigzag stitch back and forth over the raw edges of the webbing to prevent fray.) Repeat with the other side.

Born on Earth Day, I have been sewing, crafting, and recycling for as long as I can remember. I created reusable sandwich wraps to reduce the amount of plastic bags used each week and to make my lunch a little more exciting. Since creating my Etsy shop, I have expanded my work to include snack packages, lunch sacks, and produce bags.

www.sewreusable.com

www.foodstuffs.etsy.com

MADE BY
Cheryl B. Steighner

Reusable Sandwich Wrap

Finished size: 15″ × 11″

Fabric on the outside and ripstop vinyl on the inside, these quick and fun sandwich wraps that save money, reduce the use of plastic bags, and make a statement all at the same time. You will want to make several!

MATERIALS AND CUTTING INSTRUCTIONS

16″ × 20″ piece cotton fabric for exterior:

- Cut 1 oval.

16″ × 20″ piece cotton lining, such as muslin:

- Cut 1 oval.

16″ × 20″ piece ripstop nylon for lining:

- Cut 1 oval.

3″ length of oval, elastic cord

¾″-diameter button

Removable fabric pen

CONSTRUCTION

Note: *Seam allowance is ½" unless otherwise noted.*

Assembly

1. Use a fabric pen to mark A on the wrong side of the ripstop nylon.

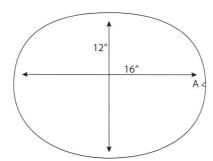

Cut 1 cotton exterior.
Cut 1 cotton lining.
Cut 1 ripstop nylon.

2. Place the cotton lining underneath the wrong side of the cotton exterior. Place the right side of the ripstop nylon so it faces the right side of the cotton exterior. Pin together.

3. Fold a 3" piece of oval cord elastic into a U shape. Keeping the ends flat, close the U to form a teardrop shape (the ends should be side-by-side, not overlapping). Place the elastic U between the ripstop nylon and the cotton exterior at mark A. Make sure the raw edges of the elastic are facing the edge of the oval and are flat against the fabric. Pin in place.

4. Sew along the outside of the oval, leaving a 2"–3" opening along one of the longer, straight sides. Stitch around again for extra durability, preserving the opening.

5. Trim the seam allowance to ⅛" near the stitching and clip the curves. Turn the wrap right side out, work the seams flat, and press into an oval shape with a cool iron on the cotton side. The elastic loop should now be facing out. Fold in the seam opening and pin it closed. Topstitch ⅛" around the outside of the wrap to close the seam opening and to give the wrap a finished look.

6. With the ripstop facing up, work from the opposite end of the elastic loop as you fold the wrap in half lengthwise. Measure 3" in from the bottom edge of the cotton fabric and mark the right side of the fold with a removable fabric pen. This will be where you will place your button. To test the button placement, fold the wrap as you would with a sandwich in it to see if the loop covers your pen marking. Adjust the button placement accordingly. Hand sew the button to the fabric over the mark.

Using your sandwich wrap

1. Lay the wrap flat, lining side up. Place the sandwich in the middle.

2. Fold the long sides toward the middle over the sandwich.

3. Fold the button end toward the middle.

4. Fold the elastic end toward the middle and fasten over the button.

To clean, either hand wash or toss it in the washing machine. Line dry.

I am an independent crafter and freelance writer living in Atlanta, Georgia, with my husband and two cats. I love working with vintage fabric and salvaged materials. There's just something about giving found objects a brand new life that really appeals to me. They lend their own stories to everything I make.

My crafty business, Glue and Glitter, is all about using existing materials in products that help folks waste less without feeling deprived. I believe in the power of little changes: using cloth napkins instead of paper or a reusable bag instead of a plastic one. Things like this add up to make a big impact! Even the act of cooking is so much greener than takeout when you consider all the packaging involved in ordering that Chinese delivery. If a cute apron encourages you to get in the kitchen and put a meal together or a lunch kit gets you packing your lunch for work or school, I hope that I can make one to inspire you!

www.glueandglitter.com

MADE BY
Rebecca Striepe

Brown Baggin' Lunch Tote

Finished size: 6″ × 6½″ × 13″

The structure of this bag is designed specifically to accommodate a stacking bento box. Check our Resources section (page 128) for where to buy a bento box that will fit perfectly. Due to the size, structure, and versatility, this bag makes a great gift for the eclectic people in your life.

MATERIALS AND CUTTING INSTRUCTIONS

⅝ yard brown fabric for outer bag:

- Cut 1 rectangle 16″ × 6½″ for flap.
- Cut 2 rectangles 2″ × 7½″ for handle.
- Cut 1 rectangle 36″ × 13½″ for outer bag.

½ yard coordinating fabric for lining:

- Cut 1 rectangle 36″ × 13½″ for lining.

Tailor's chalk

CONSTRUCTION

Note: *All seam allowances are ¼″.*

Making the Flap

1. Fold the flap fabric in half, right sides together, so you end up with an 8″ × 6½″ rectangle. Stitch both long sides.

2. Turn the flap right side out and press.

3. Topstitch around the 3 finished sides of the flap.

4. Add a buttonhole ½″ from the bottom center of the flap and press again to set the stitching.

Making the Handle

1. Put the 2 pieces of handle fabric right sides together; pin.

2. Stitch around 3 sides, leaving 1 short side open.

3. Turn the handle right side out, tuck in the unfinished edge by ¼″, and press.

4. Topstitch around all 4 sides of the handle.

Assembling the Bag

1. Fold the outer fabric in half, right sides together, so you end up with an 18″ × 13½″ rectangle; press. Stitch up both long sides.

2. Form the bottom of your bag by flattening the body, so that both side seams line up. The bottom of the bag will naturally form a diamond shape. Use a ruler to measure 2 lines 6½″ in length perpendicular to the side seams (see the dotted horizontal lines in the illustration below). Pin and mark your lines with tailor's chalk. Stitch along the marked lines and then trim off the excess.

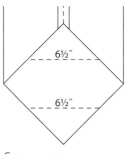

Corner seams

3. Repeat Steps 1 and 2 with the lining fabric.

4. Fold down the fabric around the top of the outer bag to the wrong side by ½″ and press. Repeat this step with the lining.

5. Turn the outer bag right side out, being careful not to let the top come unfolded. You may need to press the top of the bag again.

6. Place the bag lining into the outer bag and pin the 2 pieces together around the top. Sandwich the flap so it is centered between the lining and the outer fabric on the back side of the bag. Pin.

7. Stitch around the perimeter of the bag twice. The first row should be ⅛″ from the top of the bag, and the second, ¼″ from the top of the bag.

8. Pin the handle so it is centered on the top back of the bag. Sew a ¾″ × ½″ strong box on each edge. (**Note**: *A strong box is a rectangle with an X in the center, and it will make your bag stand up to a hearty lunch.*)

Yokomono Studio specializes in modern bags and home accessories with a Japanese aesthetic. Blend two parts midcentury modern with one part functional Tokyo subway system, and stir! All Yokomono Studio items are conceived, cut, sewn, and stitched by me in my Berkeley, California, studio. My one and only goal is to create unique, well-designed handcrafted items that make their owners happy.

www.yokomonostudio.com
www.yoko@yokomonostudio.com

MADE BY
Yoko Drain

Quilted Cotton Lunch Bag with Drawstring Closure

Finished size: 13″ × 7½″ × 5″

This bag has a fun basket-like design and an easy cinch-top closure. A sturdy exterior case make a perfect carry-all for any reusable container.

MATERIALS AND CUTTING INSTRUCTIONS

¾ yard solid-colored fabric for body, liner, and strap:

- Cut 2 rectangles 22″ × 14″ for body and liner.
- Cut 1 strip 13″ × 3″ for strap.

½ yard printed fabric for top closure and strap:

- Cut 1 rectangle 8″ × 27″ for top closure.
- Cut 1 strip 13″ × 3″ for strap.

½ yard batting:

- Cut 1 rectangle 21″ × 13″ for body.
- Cut 1 strip 13″ × 2″ for strap.

31″ length of white cotton rope (approximately ¼″ wide) for drawstring

Removable fabric marker

CONSTRUCTION

Note: *All seam allowances are ½".*

Making the Quilted Body

1. Use the removable fabric marker to draw 45°-angle guidelines on the right side of a 22" × 14" piece of solid fabric. Space the lines 1½" apart.

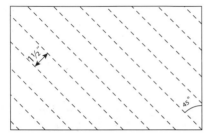

Draw guidelines.

2. With the wrong side up, place the batting in the center of the solid fabric (½" from all edges) and place pins on the *fabric side* to secure it. (The pins are visible when you quilt.)

3. Machine quilt by following the guidelines.

4. With the *batting* side out, fold the quilted rectangle in half. Stitch ½" from the edges on both sides. Make sure to backstitch at the top.

5. To form the bottom of the bag, take one of the side seams you just sewed and place it on top so the top of the bag is toward you. Force the bag to flatten, with the bottom of the seam forming the top of the triangle. Open up the seams. Stitch across the triangle as shown to make a 5" line of stitching. Make sure you backstitch. Repeat this step for the other seam.

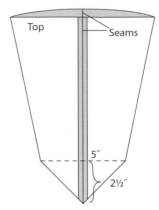

Form the bottom of the bag.

6. Trim the triangle ½" outside the stitching.

Making the Liner

1. With the *wrong* side out, fold the other solid fabric for the body in half. Stitch ½" from the edges on both sides. Make sure to backstitch at the top.

2. Form the bottom of the bag liner as you did the outer fabric, following Steps 5 and 6 under "Making the Quilted Body."

Making the Top Closure

1. With the wrong side out, fold the 8" × 27" print fabric in half, bringing the short ends together. Stitch the short sides together from the top, stopping after 1¼". Make sure to backstitch both at the top and the bottom of the short seam.

2. Leave a ¾" gap and then stitch the remaining 6" seam from the gap to the bottom. Backstitch at both the top and the bottom.

3. Press the seam open. With the print fabric *wrong* side out, press under the top edge by ½". Press under again ¾".

Make casing.

4. Topstitch along the edge of the bottom fold.

Making and Attaching the Strap

1. With right sides together, pin the solid and print strap pieces together.

2. Stitch along a long side ½" from the edge. Press the seam open.

3. Place the batting against the stitching on the solid fabric. Press the long raw edges of the solid and print fabrics in by ½". Fold the strap along the seam, matching the folded edges. Place pins to secure the fabric and batting.

4. Topstitch along both long sides ⅛" and then ⅝" from the edge, for a total of 4 stitch lines.

5. With the print fabric side up, pin the strap to the top center of the quilted body. Leave 1" at the end of the strap. Stitch them together ½" from the top of the body.

6. Repeat Step 5 on the other side. You will need to fold the body so that the strap can go around to the other side.

FINISHING

1. With the wrong side out and the casing side down, place the top closure over the body. Make sure to line up the side seam, as well as the top of the body and the bottom of the top closure. Stitch ½" from the edge.

2. With the wrong side out, place the liner over the body. Make sure to line up the side seams and the top edges.

3. Starting from the seam, stitch 1" from the top edges, leaving a 4" gap at the end. Make sure to backstitch at the beginning and end.

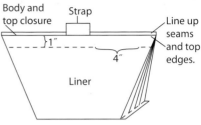

Attach the lining and closure.

4. Turn the bag right side out by pulling it through the opening made in Step 3.

5. Push the top closure into the body and pin the edges together. Make sure the 4" opening is folded in the same manner. Stitch ½" from the top.

6. Insert the drawstring into the casing. Attach a safety pin to one end of the cord and use it to push the string through the casing. Tie the drawstring ends together.

CORNER CONSTRUCTION TECHNIQUES

Many of the projects in this book use one of two basic approaches to making the bottom corners of the lunch bags. In the first approach, small squares are cut out of the bottom corners of the bag before the corners are stitched. The second approach involves pinching the bottom corners before stitching. Both techniques result in a flat bag bottom and sharp corners. The basic techniques are shown here. Please refer to each project for the proper measurements.

TECHNIQUE 1:
CUT AWAY CORNER SQUARES

1. Lay the bag front on top of the bag back with right sides together. Cut a small square out of each of the lower corners. See the project for specific measurements.

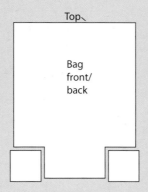

Top

Bag front/ back

2. Stitch the bag front to the bag back along the sides and bottom, using the seam allowance designated in the project instructions. Press the seams open.

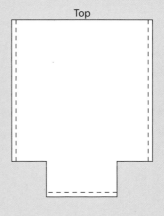

Top

3. Pinch a corner, lining up the side seam and bottom seam/ fold. Stitch using the seam allowance indicated in the project instructions. Repeat with the remaining corner.

Stitch.

4. Turn the bag right side out and push the corners out. The bag will have a nice, flat bottom.

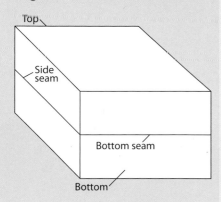

Top
Side seam
Bottom seam
Bottom

TECHNIQUE 2: PINCH CORNERS AND STITCH

1. Place the bag front on top of the bag back with right sides together. (In some projects, the front/back is one piece that is folded in half so there is no bottom seam.) See the project instructions for specific measurements. Stitch the side and bottom seams.

Top

Bag
Wrong side

2. Pinch each lower corner of the bag, lining up the side seam with the bottom seam/fold.

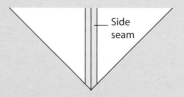

Side seam

3. Stitch across each lower corner of the bag perpendicular to the side seam. Refer to the project instructions for measurements.

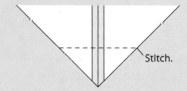

Stitch.

4. Trim the corner seam. Most, but not all, projects require trimming this seam; refer to the project instructions.

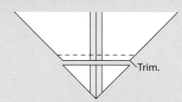

Trim.

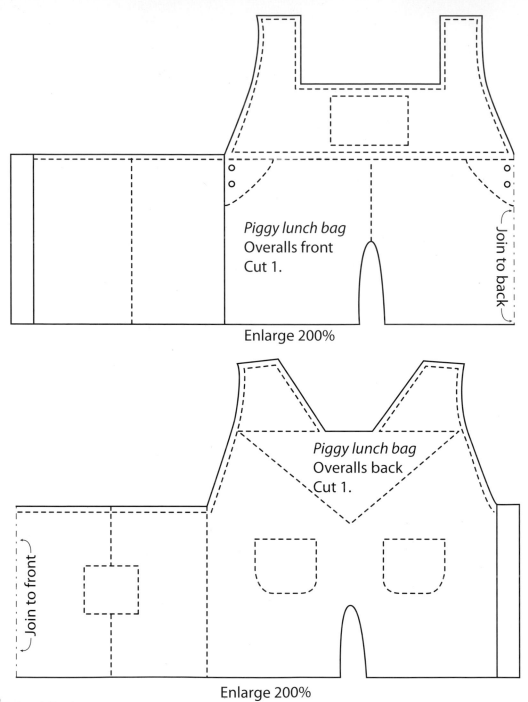

Piggy lunch bag
Overalls front
Cut 1.

Join to back

Enlarge 200%

Piggy lunch bag
Overalls back
Cut 1.

Join to front

Enlarge 200%

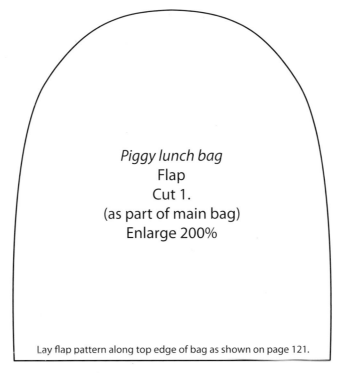

Piggy lunch bag
Flap
Cut 1.
(as part of main bag)
Enlarge 200%

Lay flap pattern along top edge of bag as shown on page 121.

Piggy lunch bag
Eye
Cut 2.

Piggy lunch bag
Nose
Cut 1.

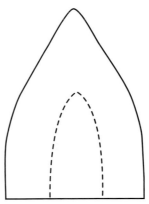

Piggy lunch bag
Ear
Cut 4.

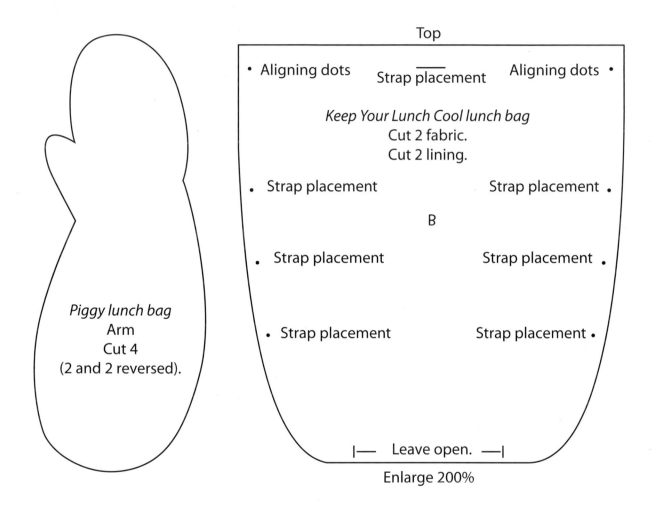

Top

• Aligning dots   Strap placement   Aligning dots •

Keep Your Lunch Cool lunch bag
Cut 2 fabric.
Cut 2 lining.

• Strap placement   Strap placement •

B

• Strap placement   Strap placement •

• Strap placement   Strap placement •

Piggy lunch bag
Arm
Cut 4
(2 and 2 reversed).

|— Leave open. —|

Enlarge 200%

*Mushroom
picnic bag*

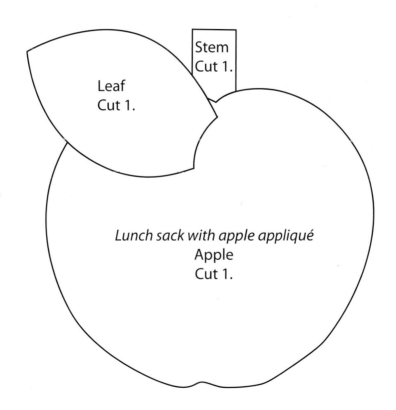

Stem
Cut 1.

Leaf
Cut 1.

Lunch sack with apple appliqué
Apple
Cut 1.

Sack lunch
Cut 4 cream felt for bread.
Cut 2 pink felt for ham.

Sack lunch
Cookie

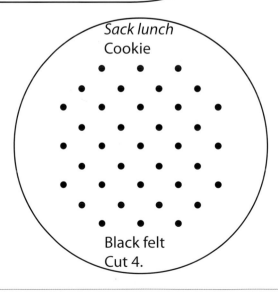

Black felt
Cut 4.

Sack lunch
Banana tip
Brown felt
Cut 1.

Sack lunch
Cheese
Yellow felt
Cut 2.

Sack lunch Cream filling	White felt Cut 1.	Place on fold

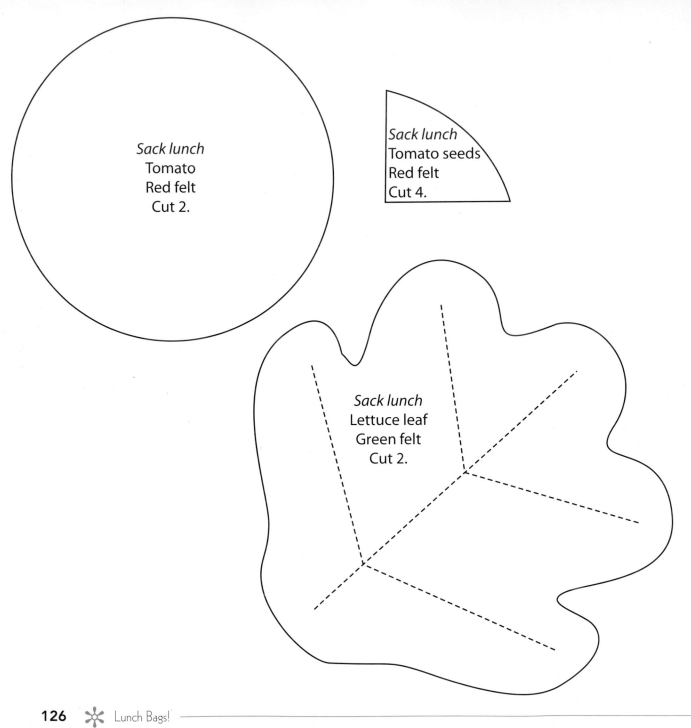

Sack lunch
Tomato
Red felt
Cut 2.

Sack lunch
Tomato seeds
Red felt
Cut 4.

Sack lunch
Lettuce leaf
Green felt
Cut 2.

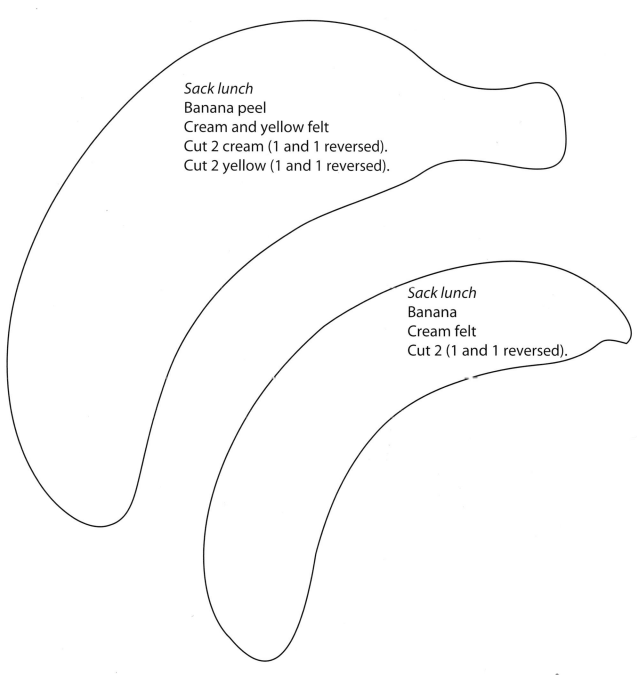

Sack lunch
Banana peel
Cream and yellow felt
Cut 2 cream (1 and 1 reversed).
Cut 2 yellow (1 and 1 reversed).

Sack lunch
Banana
Cream felt
Cut 2 (1 and 1 reversed).

Resources

Insul~Brite insulated lining
The Warm Company
www.warmcompany.com

Bento Box
www. us.locknlock.com

For a list of other fine books from C&T Publishing, ask for a free catalog:

C&T Publishing, Inc.
P.O. Box 1456
Lafayette, CA 94549

800-284-1114

Email: ctinfo@ctpub.com
Website: www.ctpub.com

Tips and Techniques can be found at www.ctpub.com > Consumer Resources > Quiltmaking Basics: Tips & Techniques for Quiltmaking & More

C&T Publishing's professional photography services are now available to the public.
Visit us at www.ctmediaservices.com.

FOR SEWING SUPPLIES:
Cotton Patch
1025 Brown Ave.
Lafayette, CA 94549

Store: 925-284-1177
Mail order: 925-283-7883

Email: CottonPa@aol.com
Website: www.quiltusa.com

NOTE: Fabrics used in the projects shown may not be currently available, as fabric manufacturers keep most fabrics in print for only a short time.

C&T Publishing would like to thank Michael Miller Fabrics for generously supplying the Lantern Bloom Collection by Laura Gunn used as backgrounds in many of the photographs.